Fields and Streams

Fields and Streams

STREAM RESTORATION, NEOLIBERALISM,
AND THE FUTURE OF ENVIRONMENTAL SCIENCE

REBECCA LAVE

THE UNIVERSITY OF GEORGIA PRESS
Athens & London

Parts of this book were originally published in different form as Rebecca Lave, Martin Doyle, and Morgan Robertson, "Privatizing Stream Restoration in the U.S.," *Social Studies of Science* 40, no. 5 (2010): 677–703, and as "Bridging Political Ecology and sts: A Field Analysis of the Rosgen Wars," *Annals of the Association of American Geographers* 102, no. 2 (2012): 366–82. Part of chapter 4 was originally published in different form as "The Controversy over Natural Channel Design: Substantive Explanations and Potential Avenues for Resolution," *Journal of the American Water Resources Association* 45, no. 6 (2009): 1519–32.

© 2012 by the University of Georgia Press
Athens, Georgia 30602
www.ugapress.org
Designed by Walton Harris
Set in 10/13 Minion Pro
Printed and bound by Thomson-Shore

The paper in this book meets the guidelines for permanence
and durability of the Committee on Production Guidelines
for Book Longevity of the Council on Library Resources.

Printed in the United States of America

16   15   14   13   12   P   5   4   3   2   1

Library of Congress Cataloging-in-Publication Data

Lave, Rebecca, 1970–
Fields and streams : stream restoration, neoliberalism, and the
future of environmental science / Rebecca Lave.
      p.   cm. — (Geographies of justice and social transformation ; 12)
Includes bibliographical references and index.
ISBN 978-0-8203-4391-4 (cloth : alk. paper)
ISBN 978-0-8203-4392-1 (pbk. : alk. paper)
   1. Stream restoration—United States. 2. Neoliberalism—United States.
3. Rosgen, David L. 4. Environmental sciences—United States. 5. Stream
restoration—Political aspects—United States. 6. Stream restoration—
Economic aspects—United States. 7. United States—Politics and
government—1989– 8. United States—Environmental conditions. I. Title.
QH76.L38 2012
333.91′62153—dc23   2012006674

British Library Cataloging-in-Publication Data available

CONTENTS

Figure P.1 Dave Rosgen. Courtesy of Wildland Hydrology.

PREFACE

In August 2003 thirty-five of the most respected academics, agency staff, and consultants in stream restoration in the United States met in Minneapolis. They were a disciplinarily diverse but otherwise fairly homogeneous group of midcareer scientists and professionals, relaxed in business-casual clothing, the shared language of science, and a high degree of personal success.

Then there was Dave Rosgen, by any conventional measure the most successful person in the stream restoration field, not to mention the room. Rosgen was dressed like a cowboy in a white hat, blue jeans, and huge belt buckle (figure P.1). He talked like a cowboy, with folksy turns of phrase that mixed oddly with the scientific jargon flying around the room. And if it looks like a duck and it quacks like a duck . . .

In the stream restoration field, Rosgen holds exactly the maverick position his self-presentation suggests. Despite the fact that he has little formal training in restoration science, Rosgen is the primary educator of restoration practitioners in the United States, and training in his approach is in many parts of the country considered preferable to a PhD. His Natural Channel Design (NCD) approach has been adopted by federal agencies, including the Environmental Protection Agency, the Natural Resources Conservation Service, the US Fish and Wildlife Service, and the US Forest Service, to the exclusion of other approaches. And it is Natural Channel Design, not a university-produced approach, that forms the primary basis of the burgeoning restoration consulting industry.

Since the mid-1990s, Rosgen's work has been vehemently opposed by many of the most prominent university- and agency-based restoration scientists in the United States, including some of those present at the Minneapolis conference. The goal was to set the research agenda for the first update to the National Research Council's (NRC) work on stream restoration in over a decade, so it was surprising that Rosgen was invited and shocking that he accepted the invitation, given the tenor of the background document prepared by the NRC.[1] This position paper was sent to all participants in advance and included an implicit but unmistakable indictment of Natural Channel Design to anyone even passingly familiar with the Rosgen Wars, which, by 2003, included most people in the stream restoration field and everyone at the conference.

The opening reception avoided any overt conflict, but within a few hours of the conference's formal start the following day the situation degenerated into one of the more excruciatingly intimate battles of the Rosgen Wars. The first session allotted participants a few minutes to formally introduce their work and their thoughts about the state of the stream restoration field. A few people used this opportunity to take mild potshots at the NCD approach and its application in practice, which was uncomfortable, since Rosgen was right there in front of them, but still within the bounds of propriety.

Things didn't really heat up until the second session of the morning with the late arrival of Matt Kondolf, a professor of geomorphology at the University of California, Berkeley, and one of the most vehement Rosgen critics. Having missed the icebreakers of the previous evening and morning, Kondolf walked in without the restraints of sociality that held other attendees at least somewhat in check and proceeded to let loose a shotgun blast of critique that sounded very loud in such a small room.

What Kondolf presented was his Uvas Creek paper (Kondolf, Smeltzer, and Railsback 2001), a powerful analysis of a spectacular project failure in Gilroy, California, and a scathing denunciation of the Natural Channel Design approach. Before and after photographs, in particular, show a jaw-dropping contrast between a perfectly manicured, suspiciously symmetrical, single-thread meandering channel and the shaggy expanse of multithread gravel bed channel that replaced it only a few months later after a medium-sized storm. As aptly demonstrated by Kondolf, the project design was an obvious disaster in the making. His conclusion — that the Natural Channel Design approach is a short-sighted, opportunistic piece of bad science — sounded like a call to the barricades. The target of revolutionary wrath, however, was located not a respectable distance away at Versailles but no more than twenty-five feet from the podium.

It was, to put it mildly, uncomfortable.

But here's the thing about the Uvas Creek case study: whatever the project's failings, its relationship to Natural Channel Design is tenuous because the designers did not employ anything close to the full approach. Uvas Creek is a telling example of the dangers of allowing poorly trained, inexperienced people to create new stream channels, but as a sweeping indictment of Natural Channel Design it has little traction. Rosgen pointed this out. Kondolf disagreed, and the conversation degenerated into barely veiled hostilities until the organizers cut it off. Both sides declared victory in private conversations, and nobody in the room changed his or her mind.

This skirmish was unusual for the sheer level of social discomfort it created, but in all other respects it was typical of the Rosgen Wars in both its substance and seeming irresolvability. A vocal university- and agency-scientist opposition has been denouncing Rosgen as a charlatan and snake oil salesman since the mid-1990s. These guardians of scientific legitimacy — bearing academic sanctification in the form of prestigious degrees, jobs, and publications — have argued against the Natural Channel Design approach in print, at conferences, and in short courses to remarkably little effect. Rosgen's classification system, design approach, and short course series are increasingly seen in the restoration field not just as scientifically legitimate but as a *more legitimate* basis for restoration practice than academically produced science and training.

This raises some very important questions about the political economy of scientific fields. What (and who) confers authority within scientific fields: knowledge, a degree from a top-ranked institution, market demand, the state? How is that changing with the global rise of neoliberalism, with its emphasis on the privatization and commercialization of knowledge? Is Rosgen's ability to supplant the university as educator, researcher, and developer of applied techniques a fluke or a portent of things to come? These are the questions at the heart of this book.

ACKNOWLEDGMENTS

Qualitative research is impossible unless a great number of busy people take time away from their primary activities to talk. I am thus very grateful both to the short course students who filled out my surveys and put up with having one of their fellow participants observe them and to the people who took the time to talk with me about their restoration work during my various rounds of interviews (interview subjects are listed by name in the appendix). Of the latter group, there are a few who were particularly generous, speaking with me multiple times to help me get a better grasp on stream restoration history, policy, practice, and science. I am especially grateful to Martin Doyle, Craig Fischenich, Matt Kondolf, Greg Koonce, Jim MacBroom, Dale Miller, Dave Rosgen, Doug Shields, and Jim Wilcox.

A startling number of people have read the dissertation on which this book is based, and dog-eared copies have been spotted everywhere from seminar rooms to conference bars. I have received more than 130 comments, many from people unfamiliar to me. These letters and e-mails were very helpful both in confirming my analysis of the Rosgen Wars and in pointing out which parts of the initial manuscript worked and which did not. My thanks to all of you who took the time to write to me.

Academic labor may be largely solitary, but academic thinking is not. The arguments that follow were honed in conversation with a number of audiences, including the Restoration Ecology Program at Umeå University and the Geography Departments at the University of Illinois, University of Kentucky, Miami University of Ohio, University of Uppsala, and West Virginia University. Phillip Mirowski and Sam Randalls have been both interlocutors and partners in crime, helping to expand and deepen my thinking about neoliberalism and the university.

At Indiana University, my fellow Sawyer Seminar organizers and participants Eric Deibel, Ilana Gershon, Tom Gieryn, Eric Harvey, Eden Medina, Elizabeth Nelson, Jutta Schickore, and Kalpana Shankar have done much to push my thinking on the science and technology studies front. I also appreciate Micol Siegel's consistent willingness to question the basic premises everyone else in the room took for granted.

To say that the geomorphology community at the University of California at Berkeley was instrumental to this project is to understate. I could not have done this research if Laurel Collins, Kurt Cuffey, Bill Dietrich, and Matt Kondolf had not been willing to take in a stray social scientist and feed her on G. K. Gilbert, Reds Wolman, Thomas Dunne, and the broader fluvial geomorphology canon. Their intellectual openness and generosity is a gift for which I am profoundly grateful.

This project also builds on the conversations, arguments, and suggestions of Joe Bryan, Jason Delborne, Martin Doyle, Mike Dwyer, Ben Gardner, Julie Guthman, Charles Lave, Jean Lave (who provided incredible feedback on multiple drafts), Tom Medvetz, Phil Mirowski, Gwen Ottinger, Sam Randalls, Morgan Robertson, Sara Shostak, Jason Strange, and my fantastic graduate school cohort: Andy Bliss, Jennifer Casolo, Wendy Cheng, Rita Gaber, Shiloh Krupar, Jason Moore, and Madeline Solomon (and our honorary cohort member, Diana Gildea). In addition, Becky Mansfield and Matt Wilson gave me a serious advice/pep talk at the 2010 Crit Mini, a pivotal intervention in the intellectual development of this book.

I was blessed with a really formidable dissertation committee. Michael Burawoy pushed me to think more carefully about the mechanisms of Rosgen's success, to read Bourdieu's work on fields, and to consider more critically what Bourdieu says about conflict. Kurt Cuffey was remarkably willing to engage seriously with social science research and very patient in explaining what to him must have seemed very basic aspects of natural science practice. In addition to providing very thoughtful feedback about the politics of ecological restoration, Nathan Sayre was a crucial source of consistent and enthusiastic support. I am especially grateful to Michael Watts, my dissertation advisor, one of the most incisive readers I have ever had the good fortune to encounter.

Derek Krissoff at the University of Georgia Press was a real pleasure to work with even when I wasn't: consistently responsive, clear, helpful, and patient in the face of unreasonable authorial stubbornness. My thanks also to John Joerschke, John McLeod, Beth Snead, and the press's graphics staff for turning my manuscript into a Real Book. Copyediting by Mary Wells smoothed out the bumps in the text, and indexing by Peter Brigaitis and Marie Nuchols made it far easier to flip through and find the good parts. Two anonymous reviewers provided feedback that was not only very helpful but also strikingly consistent, a novel peer review experience for me! The book you hold in your hands is much stronger because of their feedback.

Before I had the good fortune to connect with the University of Georgia Press, this book was almost smothered at birth by a particularly gnarly and protracted academic press nightmare. *Fields and Streams* survived to maturity because of Julie Guthman, who went to bat for me in a big way. Thank you, lady; I *really* appreciate your help.

Life is what happens when you are trying to get your research done; so is death. This project has been punctuated by the loss of people very dear to me: Elizabeth Carter, my maternal grandmother, in July 2005; Herbert Carter, my maternal grandfather, in March 2007; Henry Fienning, my brother-in-law, the day I turned in the rough draft of my dissertation in July 2007; my father, Charles Lave, the week that I filed. My daughter, Nell, the delight of my life, was born in August 2005, disrupting everything while simultaneously filling it with joy. This book is dedicated with love to each of them, and most of all to Sam: none of this would be possible without you, love.

Fields and Streams

CHAPTER ONE

Introduction

The basic premise of ecological restoration is that people can undo past anthropogenic environmental damage and contribute positively to the planet's health (Jordan 2000). This idea's tremendous appeal has made restoration a driving force in the environmental movement, an institutionalized commitment at all levels of American government, and a lucrative market. Stream restoration, in particular, has become a flagship for the restoration movement, linked to a range of issues from water quality to endangered species to recreation and drawing the lion's share of public attention.

Although the stream restoration field in the United States dates at least to the late 1800s (Egan 1990; Thompson and Stull 2002), it has been expanding rapidly since the mid-1980s (Bernhardt et al. 2005), creating a surge in demand for standards of practice and accredited training. The American university system did not step in to provide either: academics' emphasis on the complexity and particularity of stream systems (Phillips 2007) made developing standards of practice appear pointless, and as of this writing, no college or university offers a degree in stream restoration. The absence of the university system left everyone involved in the burgeoning stream restoration field — developers, community groups, practitioners, scientists, and regulators — in a difficult position. There was tremendous public demand for restoration and a rapidly expanding market but no clear source for the new basic knowledge, applications, and training needed to structure the growing field.

Dave Rosgen, a consultant with little formal scientific training, stepped into the breach by developing a purportedly universally applicable system for classifying and restoring stream channels along with a series of short courses to teach that system. Rosgen's Natural Channel Design (NCD) approach requires liberal use of materials such as boulders and large woody debris (tree trunks with their roots still attached) to prevent streams from eroding downward or migrating across the landscape. Rosgen claims that channels designed using his approach are both stable and natural, a deeply appealing combination: his NCD approach has been adopted and implemented by local, state, and federal

1

agencies throughout the United States despite opposition so strenuous and long-lasting that the controversy has come to be known as the Rosgen Wars (a name originally bestowed by one of the combatants).

While for the most part absent from university curricula, Rosgen's NCD approach is disseminated via a series of four short courses, roughly a dozen of which are held each year. Attendance at the short courses is spurred by the fact that a growing number of agencies require Rosgen training for consultants bidding on restoration projects. Professors and full-time consultants with decades of experience cannot bid on many projects because they have not studied their own subject as taught by Rosgen; in some cases, students who have completed an advanced degree in fluvial geomorphology or hydraulic engineering have been turned away from jobs at restoration firms as unqualified. Rosgen's classification system, design approach, and short course series are increasingly seen not only as scientifically legitimate but as *more legitimate* than academically produced science and training.

In response, a loosely organized coalition of academics, agency scientists, and university-trained practitioners has thrown the considerable weight of its collective scientific legitimacy into a concerted attack on Rosgen's work, determined to draw the boundaries of the stream restoration field with Rosgen firmly outside them. Critics argue that Rosgen's knowledge claims have no scientific basis, that he does not follow the norms of scientific practice, and that, far from restoring streams, his approach instead does considerable environmental damage. Despite making these arguments in a wide variety of venues — from peer-review journals to short courses to national design guidelines — Rosgen's critics have had remarkably little effect. Far from nipping him in the bud, they haven't even been able to prune him to a standstill.[1]

This unsettled state of affairs has critical implications for the health of the environment, the construction of scientific expertise, and the future of the university. If Rosgen's critics are correct, his NCD approach leads to a disproportionate number of project failures, destroying what habitat remains in degraded streams and preventing them from healing themselves. Further, because riparian corridors are a critical part of the surrounding ecosystems' health, high rates of restoration project failure could have ecological ramifications across the United States.

Rosgen's success also indicates profound changes in the construction of scientific authority. It is deeply surprising that a person with few formal qualifications and a determinedly folksy self-presentation could become the most broadly accepted expert in his field, particularly in the face of repeated denunciations from the traditional bastions of scientific authority. The current state of affairs in the stream restoration field is so far from current expectations of how scientific expertise is created that it would be easy to dismiss Rosgen as a fluke. That would be a mistake. I will argue in this book that Rosgen's success is in fact symptomatic, an early manifestation of the profound restructuring of scientific production under neoliberalism. Thus, despite the fact that stream restoration may be peripheral to your field of study, the story you are about to read has deep consequences for the public university system and the way we handle environmental science and policy across the board. So pay attention.

NEOLIBERAL SCIENCE REGIMES

While neoliberalism manifests differently in different countries and regulatory arenas, its common core has been the promotion of market-based solutions across a broad range of formerly public arenas such as health care, education, and environmental management (Peck and Tickell 2002; Harvey 2005; Mansfield 2004; McCarthy and Prudham 2004; Bakker 2005; Mirowski and Plehwe 2009), purportedly to improve public services by opening them to competition. Unsurprisingly, public science has also been a target of neoliberal policy reforms in many parts of the world, including the United States, Western Europe, Japan, and China. But another, more powerful rationale lies behind neoliberal attempts to radically reconfigure public university systems. A central tenet of neoliberalism is in fact epistemological: the claim that the market is the best information processor, the only entity capable of accurately comprehending the world. This means that academics and university systems more broadly, with their claims to knowledge and education, are at best useless and at worst actively harmful (Mirowski 2011). Neoliberal science regimes are thus driven not just by concerns about efficiency and the appropriate role of government but also by a sweeping critique of the broader project of public science.

As Mirowski (2011) points out in his magisterial book on the neoliberalization of the American university system, while science has always been beholden to its patrons, the character of those patrons matters: particular regimes of science management and funding have particular and profound impacts on the character of scientific production.[2] The practice and expectations of much of the current public-science community in the United States were shaped by a Cold War management regime that emphasized the importance of scientific excellence for national security and nation building. In the decades after World War II, the federal government thus provided sustained support for academic research and the open distribution of research results (Asner 2004; Mirowski 2011). Under this system, knowledge claims produced by those with advanced training (particularly those employed within the academy) were clearly privileged over those produced by consultants, and the market's embrace of a concept was not considered a source of intellectual legitimacy.

The rise of neoliberal science management regimes since 1980, particularly their insistence on the commercialization and privatization of knowledge, has created a decisive and substantive shift in the organization and practice of science in the United States. Perhaps the most visible change is the dramatic reduction in federal and state funding for public research universities, forcing administrators and researchers at us universities to search for private support.[3] Another widely noted impact of neoliberal science management is its aggressive promotion and protection of intellectual property in hopes of gaining commercial value from knowledge (Nowotny et al. 2005; Tyfield 2010). Even though patenting has been a losing financial proposition for the vast majority of universities (Powell, Owen-Smith, and Colyvas 2007; Greenberg 2007; Geiger and Sa 2008), the insistence on the commercialization of knowledge is only getting stronger.

A last common impact of neoliberal science management is a shift in research toward applied work that meets the needs of particular markets (Canaan and Shumar 2008; Gibbons et al. 1994; Lave, Mirowski, and Randalls 2010; and Nedeva and Boden 2006). This was demonstrated in a special issue of *Social Studies of Science* that gathered case studies from the United States and the United Kingdom on the impacts of neoliberalism on particular disciplines, including stream restoration (Lave, Doyle, and Robertson 2010), meteorology (Randalls 2010), and criminology (Lawless and Williams 2010). In each case study, researchers found that science was increasingly produced in direct response to state and market requirements as scientists were called upon to enable the new markets created by neoliberal policies.[4] This increased focus on applied work, significant in and of itself, has two additional consequences. First, it has led to increasing disputation over what can be accepted as good data, with arguments adjudicated not through the traditional mechanisms of science but simply by what the market does or does not take up. Second, it appears to have narrowed the focus of research as broader, more basic questions are shelved in favor of more immediately applicable, commercializable knowledge (Lave, Mirowski, and Randalls 2010), including the metrics used to define ecosystem service commodities (Robertson 2006; Lave, Doyle, and Robertson 2010).

The current state of the stream restoration field clearly demonstrates the impacts of the American neoliberal science regime. As I describe throughout this book, river scientists are shifting their work in response to the demands

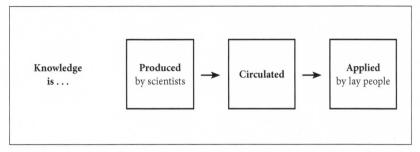

Figure 1.1 Conventional model of knowledge production, circulation, and application.

of funding agencies with increasingly neoliberal agendas, markets created by government regulation, and the rise of Rosgen, who, as a private producer of commercialized science, is himself an embodiment of neoliberal trends.

Neoliberalization does not just happen, though, particularly in an arena with as much bureaucratic inertia as higher education. How, then, can we explain the shifts in the political economy of science that enabled Rosgen's rise and the startling reversal of what had been the typical dynamics of scientific authority in the stream restoration field? To do so, we need a new model: an explanatory framework that includes both structural forces and the deeply interdependent relations among the production, circulation, and application of scientific knowledge claims.

BUILDING AN EXPLANATORY FRAMEWORK FOR THE ROSGEN WARS

The classic, commonsense model of how scientific knowledge is created and applied looks like a one-way street: knowledge is produced by scientists, who find a way to communicate it to people who need that knowledge, and those people then apply the science in the way its original discoverers intended (figure 1.1) (Goldman and Turner 2011).

Part of what makes the Rosgen Wars so fascinating is that they break up this traffic pattern: science is produced, circulated, and applied *outside of academia* and then feeds back into it by shifting scientific practice toward applied work. Further, the flow of Rosgen's work through the stream restoration field involves feedback among the stages of the model: Rosgen's knowledge claims were produced with the requirements of circulation and application in mind, and their utility in practice has led to increasing support for the production of new knowledge claims. Lastly, even a preliminary investigation of the Rosgen Wars made it clear that the limited range of participants in the classic model of knowledge transmission — scientists and laypeople — was not sufficient: both the state and the private sector were key players. Clearly, I needed a new framework that incorporated these complexities. To build it, I drew on two disciplines: political ecology and science and technology studies.

Political ecology, like the current wave of science and technology studies, dates back to the early 1980s. Initially, the field combined explanatory frameworks and research methods from cultural ecology and agrarian political economy to counter common science and policy narratives that ascribe environmental degradation to overpopulation and ignorant (or even willful) overuse by local resource users. Instead, political ecologists deploy a combination of ethnographic evidence, natural science data, historical analysis, and structural and poststructural theory to explain such degradation as a response to colonial, neocolonial, and/or neoliberal economic and environmental policies (Blaikie 1985, 1999; Blaikie and Brookfield 1987; S. Hecht 1985; Peet, Robbins, and Watts 2011; Peet and Watts 1996, 2004; Peluso 1992, 1993; Peluso and Watts 2001; Robbins 1998; Watts 1985, 1987, 2000); in some cases, political ecologists take the argument further, undermining claims that environmental degradation has, in fact, taken place (Blaikie 1985; Davis 2007; Fairhead and Leach 1996, 2003; Forsyth 2003). Although the majority of political ecologists work in the third world, an increasing number work in the first world (e.g., the work of Karen Bakker, Julie Guthman, Nik Heynen, Jake Kosek, Becky Mansfield, James McCarthy, Morgan Robertson, and Paul Robbins).

The deployment of environmental science to enable state and corporate exploitation has long been a core subject of political ecology (Blaikie 1985; Braun 2002; Davis 2007; Fairhead and Leach 1996, 2003; and S. Hecht 1985, among many others). But despite a consistent engagement with the use of science and scientific expertise as instruments of power, political ecologists have until recently focused relatively little attention on the initial *production* of that science (figure 1.2) (cf. Fairhead and Leach 2003; Forsyth 2003; Goldman 2004, 2005; Raffles 2002; Robertson 2006; Sayre 2008). This is a problem because, as I will explain in more depth in chapter 6, the same political-economic forces that shape the production of science shape its application in environmental policy. Further, the two are in fact deeply interdependent: *particular types of science enable particular types of policy, and vice versa.* The Rosgen Wars illustrate this because the ways in which he produced his knowledge claims and the demands that led him to produce them are not separable from the application of those claims in practice. Thus for political ecologists to fully understand the resource conflicts and environmental degradation at the heart of their scholarship, they

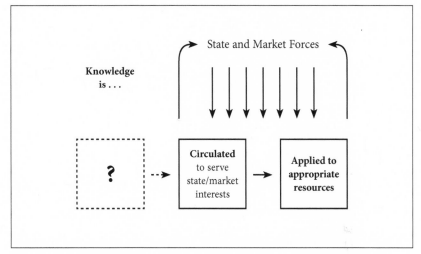

Figure 1.2 A political ecology model of knowledge production, circulation, and application.

need to examine how the science justifying particular policies was produced and in response to what forces.

Happily, there is an entire field that focuses on the production of science as a social practice: science and technology studies (STS). STS is built around the claim that science is not simply an objective mirror of reality but a negotiated product of social and political forces (Latour and Woolgar 1986). STS scholars study the ways in which science is, as Stephen Jay Gould memorably described it, "practiced within a constraining and potentiating set of social, cultural, and historical circumstances" (2000, 253). It is thus very helpful in providing a more nuanced understanding of science as not only a physical but also a profoundly social and political enterprise.

Since the beginning of the 1980s, STS has famously followed the scientist, examining the production of science as a social practice in labs (e.g., Knorr-Cetina 1981; Latour 1987; Shapin and Schaeffer 1985; Traweek 1988), medical facilities (Epstein 1996; Star 1989), science museums (Haraway 1989; Star and Griesemer 1989), the regulatory and judicial process (Hilgartner 2000; Jasanoff 1990; Jasanoff and Martello 2004; Ong and Glantz 2001), and the field (Kohler 2002; Latour 1999; Raffles 2002; Soto-Laveaga 2009). Other STS scholars have studied the circulation and application of knowledge and technology nationally and internationally (Adas 1989; G. Hecht 2002; Mavhunga 2011). But most STS authors have relatively little to say about how political-economic forces affect the production, circulation, and application of science or the relations

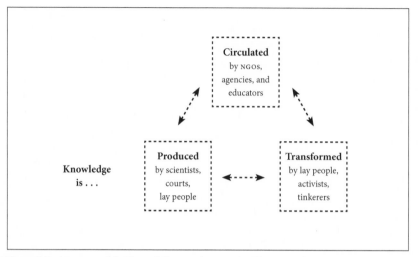

Figure 1.3 An STS model of knowledge production, circulation, and application.

among them (figure 1.3). Thus STS could not, on its own, provide a theoretical framework for understanding the Rosgen Wars either: understanding the interrelations among the production, circulation, and application of Rosgen's knowledge claims does not get at the underlying forces pushing for those claims and enabling his success.

To conceptualize the Rosgen Wars I needed to bring these two fields together (figure 1.4). This is not a new project: since the late 1990s there have been regular calls to combine political ecology and STS analyses (Braun and Castree 1998; Demeritt 1998; Forsyth 2003; Taylor 1997; Watts and McCarthy 1997). Doing so in practice has proved complicated for exactly the reason so many people think these two fields need each other: their core theoretical frameworks are quite different. The relative absence of political-economic analysis in STS is no accident; the most common approaches in the field typically draw from phenomenological traditions whose primary unit of analysis is the individual rather than focusing on the broad impacts of social structures. In contrast to this more atomistic view of society, political ecology's common sources of theory attend not only to individuals but also to overarching forces that structure society, such as global economic relations.

This incompatibility is not small, but neither is it insurmountable. The key issue is selecting a strand of STS with which to work. To date, the strongest cross-fertilization has been ontological, with geographers such as Bruce Braun,

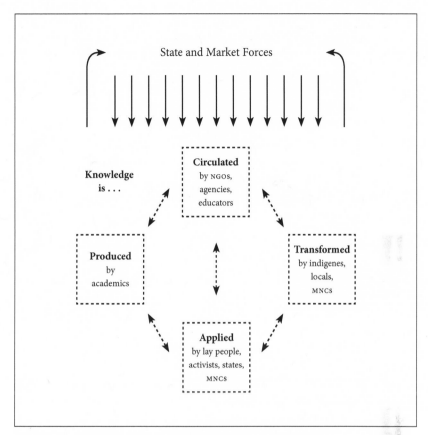

Figure 1.4 A new model for the interlinked political economy of science.

Nigel Thrift, and Sarah Whatmore (among many others) using STS to rethink human/extrahuman relations. To explain the Rosgen Wars, I needed a new bridge between the two fields (figure 1.4), one supported by their overlapping interest in the political economy of science.

In this book I build that bridge on the analytical framework of Pierre Bourdieu, whose insistence on the centrality of political economy, power, and domination makes his work very compatible with political ecologists' typical concerns.[5] Bourdieu was one of the major sociologists of the twentieth century, and STS was one of the many sociological subfields in which he participated. His primary concern was with the deeply interconnected, mutually reinforcing relations between class power and culture. He thus paid particular attention to the cultural institutions that embodied and reproduced class relations, particularly education, art, and religion but also science. Despite his enormous influence on sociology and anthropology, Bourdieu is not a central figure in either political ecology or STS. Within political ecology Bourdieu is not much discussed (see Sayre 2002; Wilshusen 2009). For its part, the STS world is profoundly ambivalent about Bourdieu. His classic 1975 article on the structure of the scientific field is included in the major STS anthologies, but his later critiques of STS researchers for taking positions that he considered too strongly constructivist alienated many who might have made use of his powerful analytical frameworks. As STS researchers begin to engage more fully with structural issues through the new political sociology of science movement, though, there has been a recent and very promising resurgence of interest in his work.

Bourdieu's key intervention in STS was also one of the first formulations of his *field* concept, which, along with *capital* and *habitus*, forms the heart of his analytical framework (Bourdieu 1975). A *field* is a bounded, structured social arena that provides a particular set of opportunities and constraints to those who participate in it: religion, science, art, and the state are the core fields, but he also acknowledged the utility of field analysis for understanding the dynamics and structure of any field of practice, from amateur boxing to beauty pageants (Bourdieu 1975, 1983, 1991, 1996a, 1996b, 1998; Bourdieu and Wacquant 1992; Bourdieu, Wacquant, and Farage 1994). To understand the specificity of a field, Bourdieu argues, focus on the forms of power and prestige (*capital*) that are valued within it and the particular ways in which it shapes the conscious and subconscious practice of participants (the *habitus* it instills).[6]

Struggle — to delimit the boundaries of the field, to determine conditions of entry, and, most especially, to define the types of capital of most value — is a defining feature of Bourdieu's profoundly agonistic (combative) field concept. This struggle takes place within the hierarchical structure provided by fields, each of which is organized around an axis whose poles Bourdieu defines as autonomous and heteronomous. At the *autonomous* end of any field are those actors whose production is controlled most thoroughly by the forms of capital specific to that field; at the *heteronomous* end are those whose production is shaped primarily by outside forces (figure 1.5). For example, in the literary field, writers with deep artistic credibility but few readers would sit at the autonomous end of the field; Danielle Steele would reign at the heteronomous pole. The relative autonomy of a field can be measured by "the extent to which it manages to impose its own norms and sanctions on the whole set of producers," including those closest to the heteronomous pole, who are "therefore the most responsive to external demands" (Bourdieu 1983, 321).

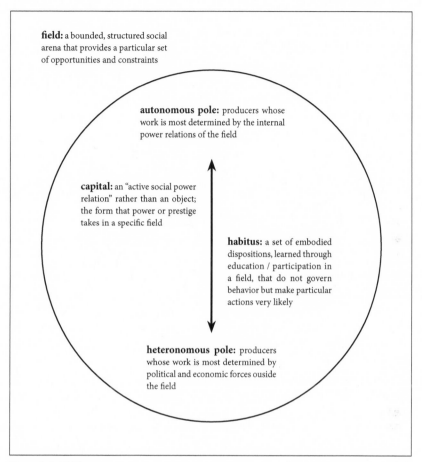

Figure 1.5 Field map.

To understand the field concept, it is crucial to grasp that for Bourdieu the positions that make up a field are analytically distinct from the agents who occupy them (Bourdieu and Wacquant 1992, 107). Thus the relationship between the *objective structure* of a field (the hierarchical and structured relations among positions) and its *subjective structure* (the habitus that agents within the field acquire through participation in it and the dispositions they bring to it) is critical to understanding a field. Bourdieu argues that these two modes of analysis — the objective positions of the field and the subjective dispositions, or *position takings*, that agents bring to it — must be analyzed together "as two translations of the same sentence" (1996a, 121). Despite this intimate analytic and actual intertwining, Bourdieu consistently argues that, once a field is established, its structure is more determining than the habitus of the individuals occupying positions within it (1996a, 105); the structural position of "sergeant" in the US Army has more effect on the person who holds that rank than the person does on the position. The habitus that agents bring with them into a field will guide them to positions that suit them, but except in extraordinary circumstances, individual agency cannot change the structure of the field itself.

Further, the internal structure of a field is particularly strong when it mirrors or manifests the power structure of the larger society in which that field sits. As Bourdieu argued in numerous contexts, social order "rests on the imposition upon all agents of structuring structures that owe part of their consistency and resilience to the fact that they are coherent and systematic (at least in appearance), and that they are objectively in agreement with the objective structures of the social world. It is this immediate and tacit agreement . . . that founds the relation of . . . submission which attaches us to the established order with all the ties of the unconscious" (Bourdieu, Wacquant, and Farage 1994, 14). Thus I will argue that a key reason for Rosgen's success is the correspondence between the subjective structure created by his knowledge claims and position within the private sector and the broad neoliberalization of the objective structure within which the stream restoration field is contained.

In one of his earliest writings on fields, "The Specificity of the Scientific Field and the Social Conditions of the Progress of Reason," Bourdieu focused on science and its distinctive structure, defined by the struggles for scientific authority: "The scientific field is the locus of a competitive struggle, in which the *specific* issue at stake is the monopoly of *scientific authority*, defined inseparably as technical capacity and social power, or, to put it another way, the monopoly of *scientific competence*, in the sense of a particular agent's socially recognized capacity to speak and act legitimately (i.e. in an authorized and authoritative way) in scientific matters" (1975, 19).

For the individual scientist, the object of scientific debate is, at the most fundamental level, to define science in order to valorize the capital she brings to the field and increase her scientific authority:

> What is at stake is in fact the power to impose the definition of science (i.e. the delimitation of the field of the problems, methods and theories that may be regarded as scientific) best suited to his specific interests, i.e. the definition most likely to enable him to occupy the dominant position in full legitimacy, by attributing the highest position in the hierarchy of scientific values to the scien-

tific capacities which he personally or institutionally possesses (e.g. being highly trained in mathematics, having studied at a particular education institution, being a member of a particular scientific institution, etc.). (Bourdieu 1975, 23)

It is critical to realize, however, that for Bourdieu the definition of science is not only political: "An analysis which tried to isolate a purely 'political' dimension in struggles for domination of the scientific field would be as radically wrong as the (more frequent) opposite course of only attending to the 'pure,' purely intellectual, determinations involved in scientific controversies" (1975, 21). Thus Bourdieu portrayed science as a deeply competitive practice in which *scientific claims and the political struggle for scientific authority are impossible to separate.*

Bourdieu's work on fields and the structured struggles that define and transform them proved to be a powerful tool for analyzing science from a political-economic standpoint. At the same time, his field framework has weaknesses that need shoring up if it is to serve as a bridge between political ecology and STS. As I will discuss in depth in chapter 6, analysis of the Rosgen Wars highlighted the overly schematic character of Bourdieu's theorization of fields and his inattention to the power of relatively uncapitalized participants.

RESEARCH METHODS AND TERMINOLOGY

I employed a variety of research methods to analyze the dynamics of the Rosgen Wars and put Bourdieu's field concept to work in the study of streams. One primary component of my research was semistructured interviews investigating the history, usage in practice, and critiques of Rosgen's approach as well as justifications for it. More than sixty participants in the Rosgen Wars — academics, practitioners, and agency and NGO staff — took the time to talk with me at length. The data from these interviews provide empirical grounding for the narrative that follows, and specific quotes from them serve as evidence throughout the book. Because of the high level of controversy around Rosgen's work, some people, particularly consultants, chose to speak off the record. A complete list of the people I interviewed at least partially on the record can be found in the appendix, along with more information about the interview process.

To see how Rosgen's work was presented and taught by opponents and proponents, I conducted participant observation at restoration short courses and conferences. I observed three of the restoration short courses that are central to the Rosgen Wars: the introductory short course led by Matt Kondolf and Peter

Wilcock in Bishop, California, in October 2004; the Level I Rosgen course held in Santa Cruz, California, in January 2005; and the Level II Rosgen course held in Fayetteville, Arkansas, in November 2006. I also attended several conferences with stream restoration strands, including the first National Conference on Ecosystem Restoration in Orlando, Florida, in December 2004. I was privileged to be a graduate student observer at the small 2003 conference described in the preface that was jointly sponsored by the National Academy of Sciences and the National Center for Earth-Surface Dynamics. I also had the rather odd experience of conducting fieldwork at sessions on restoration at the annual meetings of my own discipline, the Association of American Geographers. This part of my fieldwork allowed me to observe how the arguments at the heart of the Rosgen Wars were mobilized in collective practice. Data drawn from participant observation appear in the form of narrative descriptions and analyses throughout the book.

To delve more deeply into the motivations of short course students and their understanding and utilization of the material presented, I conducted a mail survey of participants in the Level I Rosgen course and the academic short course taught by Kondolf and Wilcock. Selected results of this survey can be found in chapters 4 and 5. The survey form can be found in the appendix.

To explore how and why Rosgen's approach is used in practice by the agencies that fund, regulate, and carry out restoration projects, I conducted a detailed case study of adoption patterns among local, state, and federal agencies in North Carolina, a hot spot of restoration activity. This material is presented in chapter 3 and the conclusion, and the structured interview questions I used can be found in the appendix.

Finally, I conducted mini–case studies of several restoration projects in California that have been mobilized in the Rosgen Wars, which allowed me to explore how the politics of the Rosgen Wars play out in practice and compare factional opinions with the physical reality of restoration projects. In each case I conducted interviews with project participants, reviewed project documents, and collected and/or reviewed geomorphological survey data. These data have deeply informed my analysis of the Rosgen Wars but are most present in chapters 2 and 4.

Given the very heated politics and rhetoric of the Rosgen Wars, I conducted all the fieldwork described above with careful attention to consent and respect for combatants on both sides of the conflict. Although the Institutional Review Board at UC Berkeley gave me an exemption for my research, I put together a rather forbidding 1.5-page consent form in an attempt to remind people that speaking on the record is serious business. As I wrote up my analysis, I sent the quotes I wished to use as evidence back to their speakers, with the text on either side as context, to be sure that people were comfortable with the material I used in publications. Further, to avoid pouring gasoline on the fire, I excluded particularly inflammatory quotes from the text that follows.

The terminology I use in this book is another part of my effort not to fan the flames. Unsurprisingly, the controversy over Rosgen's work spills over into disagreements about what to call his approach and those who use it. In the academic literature, authors typically dismiss the combination of Rosgen's classification system and design approach as the "Rosgen Method." In part to disassociate the method and the man and in part out of recognition that many key elements of his design approach spring from previous work by Luna Leopold and others, Rosgen and his advocates instead use the name "Natural Channel Design." As Natural Channel Design is both in far more common use and avoids condescension, I use it throughout this book to refer to Rosgen's knowledge claims.

Finding respectful language to refer to those who use the Natural Channel Design approach is also complicated. The level of personal devotion Rosgen inspires among many of his students has led critics to develop widely used derisive nicknames, including Rosgenites, Rosgenauts, and Rosgefarians. While these labels are certainly catchy, they are not notably respectful. A more appropriate label could be "Rosgen students," as the vast majority of Rosgen's supporters have taken one or more of his short courses, and course attendance provides a strong common bond; but not all Rosgen supporters have taken a short course, and many who have taken one consider Rosgen their colleague, not their teacher. In the interest of accuracy and good manners, I have chosen to refer them as "Rosgen supporters" or "NCD practitioners."

Similar difficulties arise in trying to label those who actively oppose Rosgen and his work. Despite a level of fervor that many will admit reaches religious levels, the opposition has not yet been graced with pithy nicknames. Characterizing them by sector as "academics" collapses immediately, as the opposition includes not only professors but also consultants, state and federal agency staff and scientists, and nonprofit staff; and, too, there are a few Rosgen supporters in the hallowed halls of academe. Characterizing the opposition by discipline as "fluvial geomorphologists" has the advantage of reaching outside the university to describe all those with a specific academic training wherever they may be employed but is inaccurate. The discipline of fluvial geomorphology, like all sciences, can be divided between basic and applied researchers, and some of the former remain blissfully unconcerned with the Rosgen Wars. Further, Rosgen opponents can be found not only among fluvial geomorphologists but also among engineers, hydrologists, ecologists, and biologists; fluvial geomorphologists have no monopoly. Finally, Rosgen teaches fluvial geomorphology, so many of his students call themselves fluvial geomorphologists. Clearly, allowing either side to claim the disciplinary title could only result in confusion.

Still searching for a descriptive label that would clarify rather than confuse, I canvassed opposition members for suggestions. Several suggested I refer to them as the "research community," but what is it that Rosgen and his supporters who test hypotheses and develop new knowledge are doing if not research? In the end, the diversity of both camps has forced me to adopt the dull but uncontested labels of "Rosgen opposition" and "NCD critics," and this is how I shall refer to the anti-NCD camp for the remainder of this book.

One final note on terminology: it will strike some readers that I have made a sudden and unexplained leap by equating Rosgen's approach — fluvial geomorphology — with the field of stream restoration in its entirety. As Rosgen's critics (and many of his supporters) have persuasively argued, stream restoration must address a broad range of factors from the physical to the ecological to the social in order to be successful. Rosgen teaches only fluvial geomorphology and hydrology; equating them with stream restoration as a whole is clearly incorrect. And yet that is exactly what is happening in many areas of the United States right now. For a growing number of people, stream restoration is synonymous with Rosgen. That is the substantive issue at the core of the Rosgen Wars.

THE ORGANIZATION OF THIS BOOK

Understanding the substantive territory at stake in the Rosgen Wars requires a basic grasp on how streams work, the ways in which human actions have degraded them, and what attempts to restore them are intended to accomplish. Chapter 2 provides this basic natural science primer on streams and stream restoration as well as an introduction to the components of Natural Channel Design, grounding the analysis of the Rosgen Wars that follows. In chapter 3 I introduce Rosgen himself and his relation to the stream restoration field's history and current power dynamics. I map out the striking shift in the internal power structure of the restoration field and describe how that shift occurred in practice through a case study of stream restoration in North Carolina.

Chapter 4 begins the explanation of Rosgen's ascent (and his critics' descent) by investigating the claims and counterclaims they level against each other. These accusations have been remarkably consistent in substance since the mid-

1990s despite the fact that some of each side's claims are clearly wrong. Even more puzzling, neither side has tried to collect definitive data to resolve the empirical questions at the core of the debate. Analyzing the debate through the lens of Bourdieu's concept of capital, however, reveals the seemingly endless loop of substantive debate as simultaneous attempts to assert authority by valorizing the types of capital each side holds: credentials from prestigious institutions, ability to abstract theoretical principles from empirical data (as in the development of models), and correspondence with the current scientific consensus versus the detailed empirical knowledge of the experienced field scientist, the practical ability to solve problems, and the environmental credentials that stem from attempts to design with nature.

At present, the second set of capital sources is clearly ascendant in the stream restoration field. This raises a critical question: how did Rosgen and his Natural Channel Design approach amass a broad-enough base of support to challenge academic- and agency-based scientists in the first place? In chapter 5 I argue that Rosgen's ability to provide the basic structure for day-to-day practice in the stream restoration field — a shared language for communication, standards of practice to enable the work of both consultants and agency staff, and the primary source of both training and educational capital — has been central to his success. I employ Bourdieu's concept of habitus to explain how the knowledge claims Rosgen has produced and the ways in which they are circulated have promoted their application so that Natural Channel Design is now central to the stream restoration field.

In chapter 6 I argue that one reason the habitus Rosgen created has had such impact is because of its correspondence with broader political-economic forces. In particular, I argue that since the late 1990s, the interrelated neoliberalization of science and environmental management powerfully boosted Rosgen's legitimacy and supported the spread of his work. Drawing on the emerging practice of stream mitigation banking, I argue that the neoliberal emphasis on market-based environmental management is both dependent on and reinforces the neoliberalization of the production of scientific knowledge claims so that to understand either we must analyze both.

The book concludes with an assessment of the significance of the Rosgen Wars for stream restoration and of the field concept as a way of bridging political ecology and STS. I argue that the Rosgen Wars are not a fluke but a portent of things to come, as the conjoined neoliberalization of science and environmental management spreads further into the environmental sciences.

CHAPTER TWO

Stream Restoration and Natural Channel Design

The Rosgen Wars are deeply substantive, so analyzing them requires a firm grasp on the basics of how streams work and why they are restored. Thus I offer here a brief primer on streams, why they have become degraded, what people hope to accomplish through stream restoration, and who is involved in the restoration process.

STREAMS AND RESTORATION

Terrestrial restoration, particularly of forests and prairies, may be the oldest form of ecological restoration in the United States (Egan 1990; Hall 2005), and wetlands restoration may be the biggest market (Environmental Law Institute 2007), but, judging by the numbers of grassroots organizations, stream restoration receives the most public attention. According to the US Environmental Protection Agency, as of 2010 there were more than 2,600 adopt-a-watershed groups nationwide, the vast majority of which focused primarily on fluvial systems.[1] This number is orders of magnitude higher than for other types of restoration (tables 2.1 and 2.2). Even assuming errors and inaccuracies in these data, stream restoration clearly holds a special place in the American restoration movement.

So why all this enthusiasm? What do rivers and streams (or fluvial systems, in more formal terms) do that so many people find so compelling?

What Rivers and Streams Do

Every raindrop, snowflake, or hailstone that hits the ground (and is not lost to evaporation or transpiration from plants) eventually ends up in a fluvial system, flowing across the landscape and at last to the sea. With that water comes

Table 2.1. Grassroots watershed restoration groups by state

STATE	WATERSHED GROUPS	OBVIOUSLY STREAM-FOCUSED	PERCENT OF TOTAL
Arkansas	15	14	93
California	222	154	69
Georgia	55	52	95
Kentucky	260	258	99
New Jersey	43	29	67
Ohio	130	119	92
Tennessee	57	49	86
Virginia	38	28	74
	805	689	86

Sources: Arkansas Watershed Advisory Group, http://www.awag.org/groups.html#able, accessed July 20, 2010; Institute for Computational Earth Systems Science at UC Santa Barbara, http://www.icess.ucsb.edu/~brenmail/wsg/att-0053/01-Watershed_Groups_in _California.html, accessed July 19, 2010; Georgia River Network, http://www.garivers.org /resources/directory.html; Kentucky Water Watch Groups, http://www.state.ky.us/nrepc /water/wwgroups.htm, accessed July 20, 2010; New Jersey Agricultural Experiment Station, Rutgers, http://njwrri.rutgers.edu/watershed_orgs.htm, accessed July 19, 2010; Ohio Watershed Network at the Ohio State University, http://ohiowatersheds.osu.edu/groups /wgp_all.php, accessed July 19, 2010; Waterkeeper!, http://frank.mtsu.edu/~waterwks /WatershedGroups3.htm, accessed July 19, 2010; private source, http://www.sklarew.com /vaflyfish/conserv/, accessed July 19, 2010.

Table 2.2. Web data on prairie restoration and advocacy groups

STATE	NUMBER OF PRAIRIE GROUPS
Illinois	6
Iowa	2
Kansas	2
Missouri	3
Nebraska	1
Ohio	2
Wisconsin	4

Source: The data were compiled through a web search for prairie organizations in the United States and in each of the states listed.

sediment, as rivers and streams gradually erode even the most soaring peaks down to Appalachian-sized stubs and wash fragments of even the hardest rock across continents to form new sedimentary layers; at the landscape scale, rivers and streams are the great levelers.

The key unit of analysis for a river or stream is not its immediate physical boundaries (as for wetlands or prairies) but its entire *drainage basin*: the geographic area within which all water drains to the same point. A drainage can range in size from a square meter in a suburban backyard to the four million square kilometers of the Amazon Basin, which is roughly the size of the continental United States.

Drainage basins are defined topographically by drawing lines between the high points in the landscape: on this side of the mountain peak (or the mole hill), all water runs to one riparian system; on the other side, water drains to a different system. Regardless of scale, drainage basins typically take the form of a leaf or a tree: many small tributaries (each a drainage basin of its own) join together into a main stem, which in turn feeds into a larger basin, creating a fractal pattern. Organisms like aquatic insects, turtles, frogs, and fish migrate up the tributaries. Water, sediment, leaf litter, nutrients, insects, and fish ride the current down through the tributary structure and out the main stem; so, too, do mercury and arsenic from mines, battery acid, chemical fertilizers, pesticides, laundry detergent, and dog poop. Thus the most basic principle of fluvial systems is interconnection: rivers and streams chemically, biologically, and physically connect their drainage basins through the gravity-pulled flow of water and the sediment carried with it. Understanding a stream requires looking at the natural and anthropogenic features of its drainage basin entire.

To get a sense of how a stream works, focus on one particular stretch of relatively unmodified channel, typically referred to as a reach. Imagine wading downstream for a few hundred meters, sticking always to the deepest part: the thalweg of the channel (figure 2.1). This path, referred to as the long profile, is one of the key things that all restorationists survey, regardless of whether they practice NCD or not. The first thing you would notice as you headed downstream would be that you could not move in a straight line and stay in the channel: unlike flood conveyance systems, fluvial systems typically curve back and forth to skirt obstacles and topographic changes, creating a sinuous pattern referred to as a meander and forcing you to wander back and forth across the landscape like a drunkard.

As you sloshed down the channel you would also notice that while the overall reach gradually dropped in elevation (this is referred to as the slope

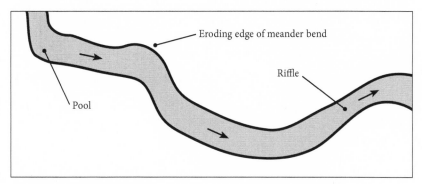

Figure 2.1 Long-profile diagram.

of the channel), it would not have a uniform depth like a lap pool. Instead, its depth would vary considerably, barely covering your ankles at some points and threatening to overtop your waders at others. The deep parts are referred to as pools, the shallow parts as riffles. If you started picking up rocks in the riffles or poking around the tree trunks and other large woody debris in the pools, you might find different species of fish, amphibians, freshwater mussels, and all manner of aquatic insects. You also would notice the variation in the surface you were walking on: the bed material of the channel. In some parts of the reach (and certainly in different reaches of the same stream) you would find sand and other fine sediments creating a smooth walking surface, while in others your footing would shift and slide on loose rock and gravel.

Now imagine picking a spot and wading back onto dry land. Once you made it out of the water and pushed through the spider webs, willows, and brambles on the banks, you would notice that the land immediately adjacent to the stream extended out in a fairly flat surface. This area, formed during floods when water spills from the active channel over the landscape, is called the floodplain. Here floodwaters spread out and encounter friction from trees and other plants, causing the water to slow, lose kinetic energy, and dump much of the sediment it carries.

Finally, if you started at the outside edge of the floodplain and walked back to the point where you left the channel, your path would likely slope gradually and inconsistently down to the edge of the bank, drop steeply down to the water surface, and then flatten again (figure 2.2); fluvial systems are typically far wider than they are deep. If you waded across the channel, scrambled up the opposite bank, and repeated your floodplain trek on the other side, you would notice the vegetation changing from moss and algae in the water to willows and

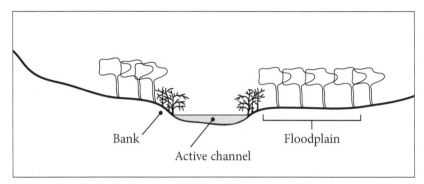

Bank

Active channel

Floodplain

Figure 2.2 Cross-section diagram.

other water-loving plants on the banks to riparian forest on the floodplain. The line you just walked is called a cross section, another central source of data for restorationists.

Left unmodified by humans, fluvial systems are dynamic over the course of a year and over longer time scales as well. For example, although for much of the year the stream flow in this reach could be comfortably contained by its banks, the annual spring snowmelt or a few days of summer thunderstorms could deliver enough water to overtop them and spill water and sediment out across the floodplain. This active seasonal connection between the channel and the floodplain is central to the ecological health of the system, providing crucial habitat for organisms at particular stages of their life cycles. This reach of stream would be dynamic over longer time periods as well, as natural erosion at the outside of meander bends and aggradation on their inside edges moved fluvial systems across the landscape, again creating crucial habitat and reshaping the landscape. Thus if you want to begin to understand a particular reach, you have to walk the long profile and a variety of cross sections many times, coming back for regular visits over a period of years.

Why would you bother? Stream systems are important to people for any number of reasons. Most obviously, without water human beings die; so do crops. Thus many of us depend on fluvial systems for drinking water and to provide irrigation for the farms that feed us. Rivers and streams are a common site of recreation, including canoeing, kayaking, fishing, swimming, rafting, and tubing. Fluvial systems provide a critical source of hydroelectric power for homes and businesses and are also home to species we value ecologically and commercially, such as salmon. Then, too, rivers flood, washing away our homes, businesses, fields, bridges, power plants, and airports or filling them with mud and debris.

Unfortunately, to reap the benefits of rivers and streams and to prevent them from flooding, we have modified them in all sorts of ways, creating a wide variety of anthropogenic damage to systems on which we are deeply dependent. If restorationists, like the Federal Bureau of Investigation, had a Ten Most Wanted list of fluvial villains, it might look something like this (no rank ordering intended):

1. Channelization: straightening an inconveniently located river or stream and containing it within reinforced banks so that it cannot migrate across the landscape, thus reducing habitat and increasing flood flows.

2. Levees: berms of packed earth or concrete built along the banks of a riparian system to prevent floodwaters from spilling out onto the floodplain, thus severing the connection between the floodplain and the channel, which reduces riparian habitat and speeds the delivery of floodwaters downstream.

3. Dams: walls of dirt or concrete built across channels to create reservoirs for use in irrigation or hydroelectric power generation, thus altering natural flow regimes, preventing the downstream movement of all but the finest sediment, and blocking the upstream migration of aquatic organisms such as salmon.

4. Removal of riparian vegetation: cutting down vegetation on the floodplain and banks to harvest timber, clear farmland, or reduce flood risk, thus increasing water temperature and removing key sources of nutrients and habitat for aquatic organisms.

5. Invasive species: nonnative plants and animals transported by humans that are capable of outcompeting native species and thus changing or even destroying existing food webs.[2]

6. Impermeable surface: paved or built-up areas such as roads, parking lots, or buildings within a drainage basin that block the infiltration of rain or snow into the water table, thus increasing flood flows, water temperature, and pollutant loads.

7. Chemical discharge: fertilizers, pesticides, mercury, arsenic, and other pollutants washed into riparian systems from many sources

such as farmland, lawns, and mines, with impacts to organisms that
live in or drink the water that range from immediate death through
poisoning or loss of oxygen to lower-level ongoing damage.

8. Diversions: canals or ditches that remove flow from fluvial systems
to provide water for irrigation or electricity generation, thus lower-
ing water levels and reducing available habitat for aquatic organisms.

9. Pipes: reaches of streams in developed areas that have been removed
from surface channels and placed instead in pipes underground,
thus destroying all habitat and increasing flood flows by moving
water through a drainage basin more quickly.

10. Construction on floodplains: building homes, crops, buildings,
airports, and even nuclear power plants on floodplains, thus creating
powerful motivations to reduce or block natural flood regimes in
order to prevent costly flood damage.

Each of these categories of human action disrupts the form and/or function
of fluvial systems, creating the harm that stream restoration hopes to undo.

Undoing Anthropogenic Damage

Unlike other types of ecological restoration, very few stream projects attempt
to turn back the clock and restore the former system exactly as it was. Because
humans have so profoundly altered conditions in most drainage basins in the
United States, in most cases there would be little point in trying to re-create an
earlier form of the channel as it developed in response to landscape conditions
that no longer exist. Instead, the typical goal of stream restoration is to restore ecosystem structure and function, bringing fluvial systems into harmony
with the current conditions in their drainage basins. Thus when you visualize a
stream restoration project, do not think of Monticello or Williamsburg, where
even the trim colors and the plant palette in the gardens supposedly re-create
their colonial character. Instead, imagine the conversion of a Rust Belt factory
into lofts for artists; even though the manufacturing industry for which the
building was designed and built is gone for good, the structure can still provide
shelter, albeit for a very different community.

Because streams connect drainage basins on so many levels, however, such
adaptive reconfiguration of stream systems is a complex business. It requires
consideration not just of changes in the supply of water and sediment and
thus the appropriate physical form of the channel but also of water chemistry

and temperature and the organisms that depend on them, including vegetation in the channel and along the banks, aquatic insects, fish, and amphibians. Ambitious restoration projects attempt to address some or even all these factors, but most projects work incrementally, planting trees along banks to shade the stream and lower water temperatures, fencing out livestock to reduce bank erosion, or removing excessive quantities of nutrients.

According to the National River Restoration Science Synthesis Project (the first and so far the only attempt to compile a comprehensive database of stream restoration projects in the United States), goals for restoration projects range widely from improving aesthetics to creating new habitat for endangered species. The most common restoration project goals are enhancing water quality (by removing excess sediment or nutrients), managing the riparian zones adjacent to the channel (by fencing out livestock, removing invasive species, or planting new vegetation), improving in-stream habitat (by adding boulders or large woody debris or removing human detritus like plastic bags and shopping carts), improving fish passage (by removing culverts and small dams or adding fish ladders), and stabilizing banks to prevent erosion (by adding some kind of material to protect the banks) (Bernhardt et al. 2005, 636).

Although the median length of restoration projects in the United States is approximately nine hundred meters (Bernhardt et al. 2005), they can be as short as the fifty meters it takes to replace a culvert or as long as the dozens of kilometers it might take to intervene on a large river. Restoration projects on big rivers are relatively rare, though, because they are much more powerful, difficult, and expensive systems in which to work. Instead, the bulk of fluvial restoration projects in the United States are conducted on streams.

That is a sadly uninformative statement, because there are no hard-and-fast rules for distinguishing among riparian systems by size. Very large systems draining thousands of square kilometers, like the Mississippi and the Missouri, are almost always called "rivers"; but so, too, is the miniature riparian system that bisects the campus of my university — "The Mighty Jordan River" — which has a drainage basin of less than two square kilometers. There is, however, a rule of thumb within the stream restoration field for defining which fluvial systems fall within its purview: wadeability. If a full-grown adult in chest waders can stand in a channel to conduct measurements without danger of washing downstream, the system is wadeable and thus a stream. The wadeability criterion means that the bulk of the projects considered to be stream restoration are conducted on systems whose active channels are somewhere between three and fifteen meters wide and that drain basins of anywhere from one to hundreds of square kilometers.

Stream restoration project costs vary widely by region, length, and goal, but median costs for most types of restoration lie within a ballpark of $15,000 to $207,000 in 2005 dollars (Bernhardt et al. 2005). Individually, stream restoration projects are small potatoes; but as thousands are completed every year, they have quite a cumulative impact economically and ecologically.

A last thing to note about stream restoration is that human goals for it are conflicted in ways that endanger the health of fluvial systems. More than any other type of restoration, river and stream projects are forced to accommodate human economic goals that directly undermine ecological goals, such as controlling flooding and preventing bank migration. For example, as described above in the Ten Most Wanted list, we have a bad habit of building housing and key infrastructure on those relatively flat floodplains, so the economic pressure against restoration of natural flood regimes is ferocious. Similarly, while unrestrained channels typically migrate across the landscape, private property does not, and owners of shrinking lots on the outside of meander bends are often unreceptive to the idea of restoring a channel's dynamism. These types of direct economic conflicts are far less common in the restoration of prairies and wetlands: once the land on which they sit is purchased, they pose few if any obstacles to human economic interests. By contrast, there are very real conflicts between human desires and hydrological processes.

KEY PARTICIPANTS IN THE STREAM RESTORATION FIELD

Some participants in the stream restoration field help create those potentially irreconcilable goals for stream restoration, others are stuck trying to implement them, and yet another set of participants is trying to run businesses despite (or because of) them. Because all these groups play significant roles in the chapters that follow, it is worth introducing them up front. For ease of discussion, I separate restoration field participants into nongovernmental organizations, clients and consultants, university- and agency-based scientists, and resource and regulatory agency staff.

Nongovernmental Organizations

National and international environmental advocacy organizations have played a huge role in the current expansion of the stream restoration field by pushing for state and federal legislation supportive of restoration. While some of these nongovernmental organizations (NGOs) have a focus that extends far beyond stream restoration (such as the Natural Resources Defense Council, the Trust for Public Land, and the Sierra Club), other NGOs focus only on fluvial systems (such as American Rivers, International Rivers, and Trout Unlimited).

At the local scale there are thousands of grassroots stream restoration groups scattered across the country that, in addition to providing an important source of volunteer labor, have been crucial advocates for projects in their communities. A few of these groups — the Hiwassee River Watershed Coalition in North Carolina and Plumas County Community Development Corporation in California, among others — have developed into influential and effective restoration practitioners, running community meetings to produce plans for their drainage basins and then designing and conducting their own restoration projects based on the priorities in those plans.

A final group of NGOs started local but have built up regional influence. Two of the highest profile are the North Carolina State University Stream Restoration Program and Pilot View Resource Conservation and Development Council, both discussed in more detail in chapter 3. Others include the Canaan Valley Institute in West Virginia and the Watershed Institute in Arkansas. These regional NGOs serve as training centers for agency staff and consultants, as advocates for restoration policies and projects, and as conference organizers.

Taken together, NGOs have played critical roles in the US stream restoration field. They help knit together the diverse participants in the restoration field and have been primary drivers of stream restoration becoming a legislative mandate, a central goal of the US environmental movement, and a practice deeply marked by contradictory economic and ecological goals.

Clients and Consultants

According to principals at the earliest restoration firms, when the client base of the stream restoration field began to expand rapidly in the 1980s, it did so courtesy of several key groups. One was private landowners, particularly the wealthy owners of trophy ranches in search of pristine trout streams whose deep pockets helped grow the market. Suburban community groups were another common client group once implementation of the Clean Water Act improved water quality sufficiently for streams to become potential amenities. A third common group of clients was private developers who, thanks to the Clean Water Act, could no longer move or culvert any inconveniently located streams on property they wished to develop without substantial investment in restoring comparable streams. A final common client group consisted of local and state public works agencies — Departments of Transportation, Water and

Wastewater Management Districts, and so on — forced into restoration to off-set impacts to streams from their projects or to improve water quality.[3]

It is difficult to generalize about the consultants serving those clients, as they are a disparate bunch. Some have advanced degrees in river science fields, while others do not have a college diploma. Many restoration firms have only a few staff members or are even one-person shops; members of a far smaller group of firms have multiple offices and regional or even national reach. Some firms focus on stream restoration exclusively, while for others restoration is one part of a larger restoration or engineering practice.

The key thing to know about restoration consultants is this: there is no national certification in stream restoration the way there is for engineers or architects. On the one hand, this throws sand in the works of the restoration market, as consultants have no simple, straightforward way to guarantee their competence to potential customers, an issue for both consultants and clients. On the other hand, it means entrance to the field is wide open, without the formidable barriers that characterize other environmental science fields; if you want to be a restoration consultant, all you need to do is hang up a shingle and start wooing potential clients. Unsurprisingly, given that there is no national certification, there is also no agreed-upon set of best practices: while Rosgen's NCD approach is currently the de facto standard of practice, it has no legal standing as such.

University- and Agency-Based Scientists

Scientists at universities and at federal research agencies make up another crucial group of participants in the stream restoration field. They span a wide range of fields in the physical and life sciences, including hydraulic engineering, hydrology, fluvial geomorphology, geology, aquatic entomology, fisheries biology, and riparian ecology. While river scientists are scattered all around the American university system, there are a few centers that are particularly known for river-related work, such as Colorado State University, the University of Minnesota, and the University of Washington. Most federal agencies with environmental mandates employ research scientists, but there are a few organizations that play a particularly visible role in the stream restoration field by providing key data on flow patterns and commonly used modeling and practical tools: the US Geological Survey, the National Sedimentation Laboratory (a branch of the US Department of Agriculture's Agricultural Research Service), and the Hydrologic Engineering Center and Engineer Research and Development Center of the US Army Corps of Engineers. In general, both university- and agency-based scientists have been hostile to Rosgen and his work, and the most prominent critics come from this group.

Federal and State Resource and Regulatory Agency Staff

The federal *research agencies* described above, though prominent participants in the Rosgen Wars, make up a relatively small part of the federal agency staff in the stream restoration field; resource and regulatory agencies contribute far greater numbers. By *resource agencies* I mean those federal organizations charged with managing natural resources in the United States; *regulatory agencies* refer to those organizations charged with enforcing compliance with federal environmental legislation. These two categories, and the individual agencies within them, have quite different organizational mandates and working cultures and thus very different reasons for adopting NCD. Yet adopt it they have, with very few holdouts.

The central federal resource agencies are the Bureau of Land Management, the Bureau of Reclamation, the National Oceanic and Atmospheric Administration, the Natural Resources Conservation Service, the National Park Service, the US Forest Service, and the US Fish and Wildlife Service. Their primary mission is stewardship of natural resources on federal or, in the case of the Natural Resources Conservation Service, private lands and waters. Some of these agencies have grant programs that fund restoration work. Others propose and manage restoration projects and issue requests for proposals (RFPs), selecting consultants to design and build each project and overseeing their work.

The federal regulatory agencies are a smaller but toothier group whose mission is to enforce federal environmental policies. The main regulatory players in stream restoration are those agencies charged with implementing the Endangered Species and Clean Water Acts: the Environmental Protection Agency, the National Oceanic and Atmospheric Administration, the US Army Corps of Engineers, and the US Fish and Wildlife Service. Staff charged with regulatory oversight can demand changes in proposed policies that would affect restoration of natural resources, set the permit conditions that require restoration, and require shifts in the proposed goals and actions of particular restoration projects. Taken together, resource and regulatory agency staff thus have an enormous impact on what kind of stream restoration work gets done in the United States.

There are obvious configurations of support for and opposition to Natural Channel Design among the federal resource and regulatory agencies.[4] Interestingly, they do not map onto the distinction between resource and regulatory agencies; their disparate missions and motivations do not translate into different positions on NCD. Generally speaking, the Bureau of Land Management, the Environmental Protection Agency, the Natural Resources Conservation Service, the US Forest Service, and the US Fish and Wildlife Service are strongly supportive of Rosgen and his work. Policies at the National Park Service, the National Oceanic and Atmospheric Administration, and the US Army Corps of Engineers vary too much by park, office, and district to be characterized. Finally, the Bureau of Reclamation, like the federal research agencies described above, generally regards NCD as insufficiently rigorous.

These configurations of federal support and critique have some very concrete effects. Supportive agencies have paid for literally thousands of their employees as well as staff at state and local environmental management agencies to attend Rosgen courses. The US Forest Service bought a copy of Rosgen's first textbook for every hydrologist in the agency, the first and only time it has made such a purchase.[5] And across much of the country, the Natural Resources Conservation Service and US Forest Service will not accept proposals for stream restoration projects unless NCD is the proposed approach.[6]

Federal agencies also play a key role in the Rosgen Wars through the preparation of national guidance documents for stream restoration practice. While not laying out codified standards of practice, those national guidance documents still have tremendous influence and are notable for their range of responses to NCD (see Lave 2008 for a comprehensive description). While two documents — the 1992 report *Restoration of Aquatic Ecosystems* from the National Research Council (NRC) and the 2007 *Stream Restoration Design* handbook from the Natural Resources Conservation Service — present a powerfully laudatory view of NCD, others — such as the 1998 Federal Interagency Stream Restoration Working Group's *Stream Corridor Restoration* manual and the 2009 *Manual 54 Update* from the American Society of Civil Engineers (Shields et al. 2009) — implicitly critique NCD by downplaying it, citing papers critical of it, and beginning the process of putting forward an alternative to it.

What is perhaps most notable about these documents, however, is their failure to provide a viable alternative to NCD. At the federal level, the dominant message about NCD is positive. NCD is strongly promoted by most of the primary federal resource and regulatory agencies; critics are primarily based in the research agencies and thus have far less control over what restoration approaches actually get implemented in practice.

At the state level there are fifty different institutional configurations for dealing with stream restoration. Typically, though, there is a department concentrating on environmental protection, and in some cases there is also a department focused on fresh water; state forestry agencies may be involved in restoration as well. In many states the biggest client for stream restoration is the Department of Transportation, required to mitigate the impacts of highway projects under the Clean Water Act.

Local offices or districts of federal agencies also play an important role in state-level restoration policy and practice, most notably, the relevant US Army Corps of Engineers district and Environmental Protection Agency regional office and the local branches of the US Fish and Wildlife Service and the Natural Resources Conservation Service. The US Forest Service, National Park Service, or Bureau of Land Management may also play a role if it controls lands within state boundaries. In coastal states the National Oceanic and Atmospheric Administration typically has a considerable say in restoration funding, policy, and regulation, as does the Bureau of Reclamation in the western half of the country. This institutional variation creates a crazy patchwork, given added color by the fact that in some agencies project managers are granted considerable discretion about the methods they require for stream restoration projects. Thus an agency's stance on the NCD approach may not be unified, and it may vary over short periods of time depending on staff turnover.

There is thus no definitive list of which states heavily use NCD. Based on my interview data and review of state-level policy documents, however, it is possible to stand back a bit and resolve the seemingly chaotic patchwork into a quilt with a discernable pattern (figure 2.3). There is a long history of support for Rosgen's work in the Intermontane West, the Central Southeastern Seaboard, and the Southeast more generally. Maryland initially embraced NCD with enthusiasm but has now backed away from it. NCD has a strong and growing presence in parts of the Midwest, while in both the Northeast and Southwest support for NCD is uneven. On the West Coast, particularly east of the Sierra Nevada and the Cascades, there are pockets of strong support for NCD, but it has never dominated in those states as a whole. It is important to emphasize that this geographical distribution is in flux; when I began my research, Maryland was a stronghold of support for NCD, and there was relatively little interest in most of the Midwest.

The staff at state and federal resource and regulatory agencies are the people charged with implementing our profoundly contradictory directives for restoration: control nature to meet human economic goals while setting it free to pursue its own ends. They are also the ones who, on a day-to-day basis, decide the outcome of the thousands of tiny battles that make up the Rosgen Wars.

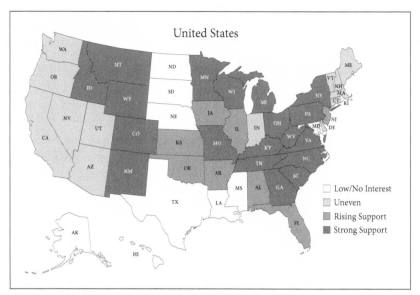

Figure 2.3 Regional patterns of NCD adoption as of 2010.

NATURAL CHANNEL DESIGN

Rosgen's Natural Channel Design approach lies at the more ambitious end of the stream restoration scale, typically reconfiguring the entire channel and often shifting its position on the floodplain. Such intensive intervention requires the use of serious construction equipment, such as excavators and front-end loaders, and as a consequence NCD projects almost always destroy any remaining habitat in the existing channel and floodplain that might have served as a basis for the channel to gradually heal itself. Rosgen and his supporters argue that this is not an issue because correct channel form is the basis of ecological recovery: if you get the physics right, the ecology will follow.

As will be discussed in more depth in chapter 4, *the explicit purpose of NCD is to design channels that both align with the natural principles of fluvial systems and are stable.* In conformity with our contradictory goals for stream restoration, a well-designed NCD project should be natural but remain in equilibrium rather than migrating across the landscape. To achieve this, the Natural Channel Design approach includes three basic pieces: a classification system, a set of guidelines for designing new channels, and a suite of recommended sub-reach scale structures for implementing those designs. While the classification system has not changed substantially since 1996, the recommended structures and techniques continue to evolve, and thus any discussion of them is limited to a snapshot of present practice.

The Rosgen Classification System

The classification system is the least controversial and most broadly used part of Rosgen's approach. The goal of the classification system is to reveal the processes at work in a particular reach through examination of its form: to "predict a river's behavior from its appearance" (Rosgen 1996, 3-3). Rosgen's classification system divides channels into alphanumeric categories based on features such as their slope, sinuosity, relationship with the floodplain, width:depth ratio, and bed material. According to Rosgen, these morphological features are relevant because they reflect the physical processes that created them and thus allow easy assessment of forces that would be difficult and time-consuming to measure directly.

His classification system has four levels. Level I depends primarily on data obtained from aerial photographs and topographic maps. The first step is to identify the form of the surrounding landscape, or "valley type," in Rosgen's terms. Valley types serve as a broad-brush system for considering geology and climatic regime as well as the position of the channel within the drainage network.[7] The next step is to divide channels into one of nine lettered categories that broadly describe their form, gradient, and relation to the valley type they traverse. An A channel, for example, is steeply sloped and relatively straight, while an E channel is low gradient, highly sinuous, deep, and narrow. These lettered designations and valley types are the coarsest level of classification.

Level II classification depends upon field measurements of slope, bed material, and overall channel form to verify the Level I alphabetical designation and sort channels into one of six numeric subcategories within the lettered categories. The primary factor in assigning the numeric subcategory is dominant bed material, which decreases in size as the classification number increases: 1 designates bedrock channels, 6 designates silt or clay. When Level II is complete, the classified reach is described with a letter-number pair, such as B3 or C4.[8] A further two levels of data collection are necessary to complete the analysis of existing conditions for design purposes, but by the end of Level II any channel's alphanumeric designation should be identifiable. That "any" is not a figure of speech. Rosgen claims that his classification system is universally applicable and that the nearly one hundred categories and subcategories encompass the entire natural range of rivers and streams.

This is not a modest claim. But setting aside for the moment the question of the demonstrability of Rosgen's claims for his classification system, the years since its first publication in 1994 have proved that for many people it has utility. Like any classification system, it allows the compression of a great deal of data. But unlike many classification systems, people generally find it both easy to apply and, just as crucially, repeatable. As Timothy Keane, a professor of landscape architecture at Kansas State University and passionate Rosgen supporter, described it, "The thing that I liked about Rosgen's classification system . . . [is that it] allows communication, because people know what you're talking about when you're talking about a c4 no matter where you're at. And it's quantitative and replicable, so that somebody in Tennessee can use the same method to measure and assess a stream that we use in Kansas or Colorado or Wyoming."[9]

Rosgen's simple designations allow visualization of complex channels. Say "B3" to a trained practitioner, and he will know that you are talking about a not particularly sinuous, relatively wide and shallow, predominantly cobble-bed, riffle-dominated system running through a narrow, moderately steep valley. Or say "c4," and the trained practitioner will visualize a predominantly gravel-bed riffle/pool system, highly sensitive to disturbance with a well-developed floodplain running through a wide, gently sloped valley. These longer verbal descriptions are themselves compressions of pages of field data and days, perhaps even weeks, of surveying and measurement.

To a research scientist or a consultant on a multiyear project trying to understand a river system, there is no substitute for the raw data; too much of the specificity of a system is lost as its description is pared down to a letter-number pair. But in a conversation between NCD practitioners about a stream system one of them has not seen, the wealth of data contained in that pair can be a very useful tool.

All but one of the restoration practitioners critical of NCD I interviewed could apply the Rosgen classification system, and almost everyone I talked to agreed that it has been very useful in establishing a basis for communication among the widely disparate disciplines involved in stream restoration.[10] In today's academic climate, interdisciplinary communication is an uncontroversial good on par with motherhood and apple pie. However, classification systems are not simply ideas, perceptions of the structure of nature that live in the realm of the mind. They have material force (Bowker and Star 1999, 39). The categories in Rosgen's classification system exert their material force in a number of ways but most powerfully through their impact on restoration design.

The Natural Channel Design Approach

When Rosgen first started teaching and implementing restoration projects in the mid-1980s, his description of his design process in short courses and papers was not exactingly specified. In response to confused students and outside criticism, he developed a precisely described forty-step design approach (at which point he was promptly smacked by his critics for producing a restoration "cookbook," as described in chapter 4). Rosgen's chapter in the 2007 NRCS *Stream Restoration Design* handbook is the first place that his design process was made publicly available. In the chapter Rosgen divides his approach into eight phases, of which the forty-step process specifies all but the first. These eight phases are:

Phase 1. Clearly and concisely define the project's objectives, be they related to physical, chemical, biological or human goals.

Phase 2. Develop or verify regional curves for geomorphic, hydrologic, and hydraulic data; determine valley types and stream classifications; obtain reference reach data.

Phase 3. Assess the stability and sediment supply of the restoration reach in relation to its watershed to determine the cause and direction of change or impairment.

Phase 4. Seek a passive solution, such as a change in land use management. If none is available, move on to Phase 5.

Phase 5. Combine all of the data gathered in the previous steps. Based on this data, complete a design and test its compatibility with the hydraulic and sediment regimes in the watershed.

Phase 6. Select and design appropriate enhancement and stabilization structures, such as cross-vanes, W-weirs, or j-hooks.

Phase 7. Implement the design, including daily construction supervision.

Phase 8. Develop and implement a plan for monitoring and maintenance. (NRCS 2007, 11-1–11-2)

The most distinctive features of Rosgen's approach appear in Phase 2: the emphasis on bankful discharge and regional curves, reference reaches, and dimensionless ratios. *Regional curves* describe empirically derived relations within a given hydrophysiographic province between drainage basin area and channel mean depth, width, cross-sectional area, and discharge.[11] Regional curves are critical to Natural Channel Design, laying out a set of regionally specific relations that determine stream classification and guide restoration design. A key feature of regional curves is their reliance on the concept of *bankful discharge*, Wolman and Miller's (1960) classic insight that the discharge that controls channel form is not the rare big flood but the smaller, more regular flow that fills the active channel without spilling out onto the floodplain — the bankful flow. In Rosgen's approach, physical indicators of bankful and regional curves are used together to determine the bankful elevation and discharge of a given reach and are critical to proper channel classification; in areas where there are no reliable physical indicators of bankful discharge, regional curves are used alone. Thus regional curves are essential for employing the NCD approach.

Once the current form of the project reach is classified and its potential form determined via examination of the reach, historic aerial photographs, and conditions upstream and downstream (Rosgen 1996, 6-5), Rosgen practitioners go in search of *reference reach* data that correspond to the project channel's classification, valley type, and sediment and flow regimes. The reference reach approach is not unique to Rosgen. In his formulation, however, the goal is not a single pristine reach to serve as a natural template but as many examples as possible of comparable reaches that are stable in order to provide a range of values to use in design. The possibility of finding and also of constructing stable stream channels is a cornerstone of Rosgen's approach and also a major target of criticism (as discussed in chapter 4).

Once collected, the reference reach data ranges are converted into scale-neutral, *dimensionless ratios*, a third key feature of Rosgen's approach. These dimensionless ratios allow designers to use data from reference reaches with quite different drainage basin sizes to guide design for the project reach. Once the overall form of the project reach is determined, the Natural Channel Design approach turns to the specific subreach scale techniques needed to implement the design.

Restoration Techniques

The most frequent adjectives with which Rosgen modifies the noun "engineer" all mean "idiot," although he has toned his language down over the years. He has built his career critiquing the traditional practice of hydraulic engineering as embodied in the work of the US Army Corps of Engineers and the standards of practice codified by the American Society of Civil Engineers. Despite this, Rosgen's approach shares a key goal with traditional engineering: stabilize the channel to prevent it from migrating laterally or downcutting. To achieve the former, the restoration design must protect the outer edges of meander bends, where the lateral erosive force of the channel concentrates; to achieve the latter, the design needs to slow the water flow enough to prevent incision without critically reducing the stream's ability to transport sediment.

Shared ends unsurprisingly lead to a commonality of means. There is a clear kinship between the traditional tools of American hydraulic engineers — weirs and bank-armoring materials such as concrete, riprap (large rocks), or gabions (metal cages with smaller rocks inside) — and the suite of techniques that Rosgen has developed. The family resemblance lies in function, not form: Rosgen's structures are built from locally available boulders and logs with roots and branches still attached. They thus have a much more natural appearance than the typical US Army Corps of Engineers project. They also exert less complete control than a straightened, concrete-lined trapezoidal flood conveyance system, although they perform much of the same work: preventing channel migration by dissipating the energy of the water flow directed at the bank or armoring the outside of meander bends and preventing incision by reducing shear stress. When placed correctly in appropriate stream systems, Rosgen's structures, like the traditional engineering structures they replace, seem to do a reasonable job of locking in a channel: *Natural Channel Design should not be confused with letting a channel behave naturally.*

Unlike traditional engineering structures, however, Rosgen's structures have aesthetic and biological goals as well — creating a more natural appearance and improving fish habitat — and it is here that Rosgen's approach departs most notably from the past practice of hydraulic engineering in America.[12] All of Rosgen's recommended structures are designed with natural materials in order to harmonize with their surroundings. These structures are intended not simply to divert water flow away from the outside edge of meander bends but also to concentrate that flow to maintain scour pools, providing critical deepwater fish habitat. The log revetments, designed with rootwads facing out into the stream, not only armor the bank but also are intended to provide shade and cover, primarily for game fish; much of Rosgen's work comes from private clients who wish to restore or create trout fisheries.

Rosgen's Three Forks Ranch project on the Little Snake River in Colorado, for example, used more than five hundred structures to maintain pools crucial for trout habitat in support of a commercial trout-fishing operation. The resultant step/pool system is probably not representative of what would naturally occur in this upper-montane valley; most likely the system historically was full of willows, beaver, and multithread channels.[13] But there is far more to the system, aesthetically and ecologically, than there would have been had the channel been designed as a flood conveyance system according to traditional hydraulic engineering principles, and that is a notable improvement over what used to pass as business as usual in river work in the United States.

CONCLUSION

The health of rivers and streams is critical ecologically and economically. Much of the US (and the world) population depends on fluvial systems for water to drink, wash, generate power, and irrigate crops. Rivers and streams provide critical (sometime frustrating) links between regions, connecting economies through water-based transport while distributing the chemical consequences of mining and large-scale commercial agriculture downstream. When we remove riparian vegetation, we reduce streams' ability to filter out pollutants that harm the health of humans and organisms we value, such as salmon. When we build new parking lots, straighten streams, put them in pipes, and cut them off from their floodplains, we cause "natural" disasters for our downstream neighbors.

If we can learn to undo these anthropogenic harms and make stream restoration work, it would be a great gift to both human and extrahuman nature. The stakes in the Rosgen Wars are thus very high indeed.

CHAPTER THREE

The History of Stream Restoration and the Rise of Rosgen

Rosgen's work and Natural Channel Design are pretty much
the standard here. If you talk about stream restoration,
that's the rule.
— DAVID PHLEGAR, water quality supervisor,
Greensboro, North Carolina

With a basic understanding of how streams work and a grasp on the primary components of the Natural Channel Design approach, we can now jump into the stream restoration field and raise some key questions about the conflict that has convulsed it since the mid-1990s. Where did Dave Rosgen, the producer of these controversial knowledge claims, come from? How do he and his work relate to the longer history of the stream restoration field? How has their entrance into the field changed it? What does the broad adoption of Natural Channel Design look like in practice?

I answer these questions through a brief history of Rosgen's professional career and of the American stream restoration field more broadly. Using snapshots of the field from the mid-1990s and mid-2000s, I map out changes in its internal power structure as Rosgen moved from a midlevel participant to the pinnacle of the field. I conclude with a case study of North Carolina, a national center of restoration and of NCD adoption, to give a sense of how strongly influential Rosgen and his work can be.

DAVE ROSGEN AND THE HISTORY OF STREAM RESTORATION IN THE UNITED STATES

Rosgen joined the US Forest Service in 1965 after completing a bachelor of science degree in forestry and watershed management at Humboldt State University.[1] Over the next ten years, he worked as a forest hydrologist on the Clearwater National Forest in Idaho and the Beaverhead and Lolo National Forests in Montana before returning to Idaho to work on the Kaniksu National Forest. In 1975 he took over the forest hydrologist job on the Arapaho and Roosevelt National Forests in Colorado, and there he stayed until 1985.

Having regularly fished in the Clearwater National Forest as a child, he was shocked by the changes he saw when he returned there in 1965. He described it in the Level I course I attended in January 2005:

> After I went to college, I went back to the very ranger district, right on those tributaries below the Bungalow Ranger Station. You didn't have to pack in anymore, you could drive right up. The Clear River was wider, shallower, and sandy. I looked upstream and saw huge swathes of clear-cuts and road failures. . . . I went and yelled at the ranger for allowing so much damage, but he said that anything we do is minor compared to Mother Nature. That's when I realized I was part of a pecking order. I was a peckee, and you know what that made him. I was an ineffective, frantic booger until I realized what I needed: data. Without the data, it's just an opinion.

There was no handbook for the kinds of questions Rosgen wanted to answer about why some streams could experience severe disturbance without taking substantial damage while other streams in the same watershed were profoundly affected. So he began to teach himself, reading, measuring, and talking to everyone he could get to sit still and listen, most notably geomorphologist Luna Leopold, whom he went to see in 1968 with data from his work on the Beaverhead Forest in Montana. During these years with the US Forest Service, Rosgen developed the core of his classification system and design approach, refining them in consultation with Leopold, Lee Silvey (his supervisor on the Arapaho and Roosevelt National Forests), and other forest hydrologists.

In 1984, while working as a forest hydrologist on the Arapaho and Roosevelt, Rosgen was asked to do work that he considered unethical. He refused to do it, and in response the regional forester issued him a directed reassignment (an involuntary transfer) to a forest to which he knew Rosgen was unwilling to go. Rosgen duly refused the reassignment. Technically, he resigned; effectively, he was fired. Regardless of what you call it, after twenty years with the US Forest Service Rosgen was out of a job and at loose ends.

This situation seems to have lasted for no more than five minutes before his phone started ringing; luckily for Rosgen, the restoration field was just beginning its current period of rapid expansion, and the demand for knowledgeable practitioners and for the training to create them was taking off. By 1986 he was teaching short courses at the University of Nevada–Reno, the US Forest Service had been forced to hire him back on a consulting basis for the pivotal Division I water rights case (Gordon 1995), and he had embarked on some of his first big restoration projects for private clients in Colorado.

The stream restoration field into which Rosgen jumped got its start nearly a century before the current deluge of public interest and has gone through a number of shifts in size and focus. In the latter part of the nineteenth century, participants worked to improve game fish habitat through the placement of in-stream structures. At first, a substantial number of these habitat improvement projects were designed and implemented by wealthy private landowners. Starting in the 1930s, however, the field swelled as habitat improvement transformed into a predominantly public project conducted by state resource agencies, the Civilian Conservation Corps (CCC), the US Forest Service, and the US Fish and Wildlife Service (Thompson and Stull 2002).[2]

The 1930s were a key decade for the stream restoration field in a number of ways. Scientists at the University of Michigan produced some of the first widely utilized knowledge claims about restoration in the form of guidance documents promoting the use of in-stream structures. Agency-based scientists also weighed in, as the US Forest Service published its first handbook on habitat structures (Arthur 1936). These university- and agency-produced guidance documents were timely, as the 1930s were also notable for the sheer numbers of structures constructed. The Civilian Conservation Corps, for example, "improved" more than 7,950 kilometers of streams and built more than 31,000 in-stream structures between 1933 and 1936 alone (Thompson 2005, 38).

As New Deal programs phased out, however, the flow of participants, projects, and funds into the stream restoration field dried up. This contraction was exacerbated by a federal policy framework that emphasized the economic, rather than the environmental, aspects of river management during most of the twentieth century: flood control, hydropower, irrigation, and navigability to improve trade. By the 1970s there were 33,353 kilometers of rivers and streams channelized and 9,490 kilometers of levees constructed by the US Army Corps of Engineers and the Natural Resources Conservation Service (Riley 1998, 220); the Bureau of Reclamation alone had constructed more than six hundred dams.[3] This rampant interference with riparian systems and the rise of environmentalism sparked a countermovement. Opposition to traditional hydraulic engineering and primarily economic approaches to rivers began in the United States in the late 1960s and spread globally (Brookes 1988, 20).

Support for the new activist and environmentalist orientation of the stream restoration field came from a number of sources. On the geomorphology front, some of the most influential work of the twentieth century was done in the 1950s and 1960s by US Geological Survey and academic scientists such as Luna Leopold, Thomas Maddock, John Miller, and Gordon Wolman. Their work had enormous impact on restorationists' understanding of natural channel processes. Then in 1967 ecologists working for the Wisconsin Department of Natural Resources published new guidelines for managing trout habitat that for the first time emphasized a holistic approach to riparian systems rather than simply plunking down in-stream habitat structures (White and Brynildson 1967).

The federal government played a crucial enabling role in the expansion and reorientation of the stream restoration field through environmental legislation in the late 1960s and early 1970s. In 1968 the Wild and Scenic Rivers Act put forward the first noneconomic view of rivers at the federal level, declaring that "the established national policy of dam and other construction at appropriate sections of the rivers of the United States needs to be complemented by a policy that would preserve other selected rivers or sections thereof in their free-flowing condition to protect the water quality of such rivers and to fulfill other vital national conservation purposes."[4] This startling departure from the traditional view of highest and best use of water resources was followed in short order by the National Environmental Policy Act in 1969, the Federal Water Pollution Control Act in 1972 (retitled the Clean Water Act in 1977), and the Endangered Species Act in 1973.

The earliest stream restoration and bioengineering consulting firms were established in the late 1970s and early 1980s just as this landmark environmental legislation began to be fully implemented. The stream restoration groups at Philip Williams & Associates on the West Coast and Milone & MacBroom in the Northeast were established in the late 1970s.[5] Inter-Fluve, Inc., opened its doors in the Northwest in 1982, as did Robbin Sotir & Associates, Inc., in the Southeast. With the exception of Robbin Sotir, who had extensive training in soil bioengineering in Europe, the pioneering group of stream restoration consultants found themselves with little explicit guidance about what might or might not work. Consultant James MacBroom said that when he started researching more natural approaches to channel design in the late 1970s and early 1980s, he "found that there really wasn't what we think of as design guides or manuals on how to design a channel for something other than a rigid boundary, prismatic type of geometry. On my own I discovered writings by Luna Leopold, other USGS people, and Gordon Wolman dealing with fluvial geomorphology. But it was never a design manual."[6] Early practitioners used the work of Leopold, Wolman, and others as their core knowledge about how natural

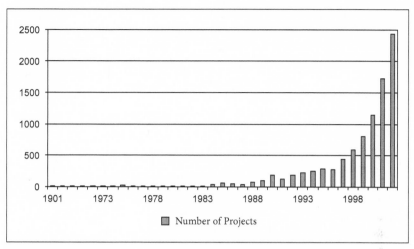

Figure 3.1 Number of stream restoration projects in the United States per year based on the NRRSS database.[7]

channels work but had to develop their own applications of these principles for the specific demands of restoration work.

As described in the previous chapter, these consulting firms' initial clients came in three main groups: private landowners, particularly the wealthy owners of trophy ranches in search of pristine trout streams; suburban community groups eager to convert streams into local amenities; and private developers forced by section 404 of the Clean Water Act to offset damage to streams on property they wished to develop by paying for or restoring comparable streams.[8] These three sources, combined with spending by federal agencies such as the Natural Resources Conservation Service and the US Forest Service, got the stream restoration market up and running.

As documented by the National River Restoration Science Synthesis Project, there was an initial jump in restoration projects in the early 1980s, just before Rosgen left the US Forest Service and set up shop as a restoration designer and educator. This was followed by more than ten years of slow but steady growth and then a much steeper growth curve from the mid-1990s on (figure 3.1). Growth in the dollars expended on restoration has shadowed the number of projects. The restoration market hit the $1 billion per year mark in 1995 and continues to grow rapidly (Bernhardt et al. 2005).[9]

Clearly, the stream restoration field is going through dramatic changes. How has this rapid period of growth and the entrance of Rosgen and his NCD approach changed the internal power relations of the field?

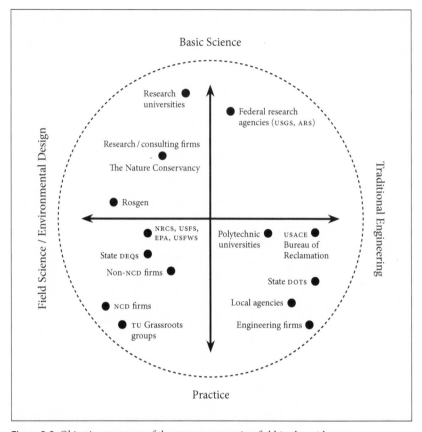

Figure 3.2 Objective structure of the stream restoration field in the mid-1990s.

THE CHANGING POWER STRUCTURE OF THE STREAM RESTORATION FIELD

Bourdieu describes the internal power relations of a field as its *objective struc-ture*: a system of necessities and constraints that exists independently of the will and recognition of participants in the field. An amateur scientist may believe she has the same right to funding and media exposure as someone who has earned a doctorate from MIT, but that belief will not get her grants from the National Science Foundation or coverage in the *New York Times*; the objective structure of power relations in her field exists whether she chooses to acknowl-edge it or not. So what is the current objective structure of the stream restora-tion field? What are the axes that structured it before Rosgen's rise, and how have they shifted? Which institutions held positions of power in the mid-1990s, and where are they in the hierarchy of the field now?

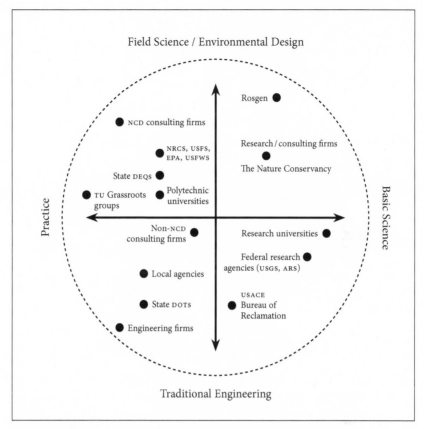

Figure 3.3 Objective structure of the stream restoration field in the mid-2000s.

The Power Structure of Stream Restoration in the Mid-1990s

As described above, university- and agency-based scientists rose steadily in status in the stream restoration field starting roughly in the mid-1930s; by the 1970s they sat at the pinnacle of the field and maintained that dominant position through the early to mid-1990s (figure 3.2). The highest positions in the hierarchy belonged to those ecologists, hydraulic engineers, and geomorphologists whose work was seen as the most scientific and economically disinterested, that is, the farthest removed from the practical exigencies and politics of restoration work. University-based scientists thus enjoyed somewhat higher status than those in the research branches of the federal agencies, such as the US Geological Survey and the Agricultural Research Service of the US Department of Agriculture (USGS and ARS in figures 3.2 and 3.3). Practitioners were relegated to the bottom of the hierarchy, mimicking the basic/applied split typical of scientific fields. The stream restoration field's secondary axis marked a different division, running from those focused on following natural principles to those focused on asserting human control through hydraulic engineering.

Rosgen was increasingly visible in the field but not yet dominant: the initial publication of his classification system in *Catena* in 1994 drew much attention, and his work was promoted in the 1992 National Research Council report on aquatic ecosystem restoration. A few consultants, academics, and agency-based scientists were beginning to view him as a threat (Gillilan 1996; Kondolf 1995), but many were unaware of him.

Federal resource and regulatory agencies, such as the Natural Resources Conservation Service and the Environmental Protection Agency (NRCS and EPA in figures 3.2 and 3.3), held a central but not dominant position in the stream restoration field in the mid-1990s. They paid more attention to working with nature and environmental values than the bastions of hydraulic engineering, such as the US Army Corps of Engineers (USACE in figures 3.2 and 3.3), which had been forced to accept restoration as part of its mission but was not notably embracing it.[10] Still, many practitioners relied on the sediment transport models produced by the Hydrologic Engineering Center of the Corps, so it was far from the bottom of the hierarchy.

As in any field at any time, the majority of participants in the stream restoration field in the mid-1990s did not hold substantial amounts of individual power (collectively, they held a great deal of power, as I will argue in chapter 6) and thus made up the lower tiers of the field. A large part of this group consisted of the agency and nonprofit staff in charge of funding, managing, and regulating stream restoration projects while simultaneously juggling profoundly contradictory directives for restoration.

Another group mostly found in the bottom half of the stream restoration field in the mid-1990s were the practitioners, primarily employees at private consulting firms but also state and federal resource agency staff involved in design and implementation of stream restoration projects, most notably at the US Army Corps of Engineers and Natural Resources Conservation Service. Among NGOs, the Nature Conservancy and Trout Unlimited both designed and conducted substantial numbers of restoration projects in the mid-1990s.

Among practitioners, the larger science/practice divide that structured the field as a whole repeated itself. The handful of consulting firms and NGOs, such as the Nature Conservancy, which had large numbers of PhD scientists on staff and functioned effectively as auxiliary research units, held more prestige than the far larger group of consulting firms and nonprofits whose work had more practical ambitions. In the mid-1990s non-NCD firms had an advantage over those that based their work on NCD. The non-NCD firms, such as Inter-Fluve and Philip Williams & Associates, were better established, there were more of them, and they were bigger: while there were consulting firms that relied on Rosgen's work in the early to mid-1990s, they were few in number outside of Maryland, North Carolina, and the Rocky Mountain states. Even in those early NCD strongholds, firms that used Rosgen's approach tended to be quite small, often sole practitioners.

The Power Structure of the Stream Restoration Field in the Mid-2000s

By the mid-2000s the stream restoration field had reoriented dramatically (figure 3.3) as Rosgen's NCD approach became the most commonly used method for restoring wadeable streams in the United States and the majority of practitioners came to look to Rosgen for theory, applications, and training. The subsidiary axis structuring the stream restoration field in the 1990s became the primary axis, as those whose work was based on the principles of hydraulic engineering lost power in relation to those whose work was based on field science and environmentalist ideals, as typified in the Natural Channel Design movement. The consulting firms and public agencies dominated by engineers — such as federal and state Departments of Transportation, water and stormwater management districts, and even the Bureau of Reclamation — started to shift toward more environmentally friendly positions in response but still occupied the lower tiers of the field.

As the stream restoration field expanded exponentially in the late 1990s, the number of consulting firms grew, finding clients not only among federal and state agencies and private landowners but also among local sewer and water districts forced into restoration in order to meet water quality standards set by the Clean Water Act. By the mid-2000s there were NCD-based firms with regional and even national reach, such as Buck Engineering, J. F. New, KCI, and Stantec. A number of consultants who were early critics of the NCD approach were forced to swallow their pride and attend Rosgen courses to maintain their client base. Others, particularly sole practitioners, simply left the field because it was so hard to find clients who would accept a non-NCD approach.

Another change was the rapid growth of NGOs promoting stream and watershed restoration. Although Trout Unlimited cut way back on its in-house restoration practice as increasing regulatory oversight complicated volunteer-based projects, local groups more than filled the gap.

And what of the formerly ascendant university- and agency-based scientists? Because of the hierarchical nature of fields, shifts in power do not come through expansion of the top tier but through displacement. Thus those who stood at the pinnacle of the field in the early to mid-1990s were cast not just aside but *down* by the rise of NCD.

What did the power shift mapped out above look like on the ground? How did the changed dynamics of the field manifest in daily practice? One way to investigate this is to focus in on stream restoration in a particular state — North Carolina — where a well-integrated and highly motivated community of regulatory and resource agency staff, Clean Water Act requirements, and strong local institutions helped the state become both a hot spot of stream restoration and a national center of Natural Channel Design.

STREAM RESTORATION IN NORTH CAROLINA

In the early 1990s North Carolina developed a strong water quality program in response to Clean Water Act requirements, but it focused only on wetlands, and many of the agency staff involved in the program were increasingly concerned that the program was neglecting streams.[11] This concern intensified in 1996, when the state Department of Transportation was required to mitigate impacts to streams for the first time (previously, mitigation had only been required for wetlands). As Brian Bledsoe, former nonpoint source program coordinator for North Carolina, described it, "there was a relatively strong and advanced water quality program [in North Carolina], and . . . I think we were kind of at a tipping point. We'd been working on wetlands a lot, but there was this group of us there who got out walking streams and thinking about how we managed water quality and concluded that we really needed to integrate a geomorphic perspective."[12]

Rosgen taught his first class in North Carolina in 1996 just as the agency community began to search for more geomorphic approaches to fixing damaged streams. As shown in figure 3.2, Rosgen did not yet enjoy the national stature he does today, and NCD was not yet the de facto national standard of practice. But his work addressed a pressing need and had tremendous and immediate appeal. The North Carolina agency community embraced NCD and was instrumental in promoting its circulation and application throughout the South.

Angela Greene, a Natural Resources Conservation Service engineer and strong Rosgen advocate, described how she had been working on streams from a more conventional engineering approach for years, and then

I went on a detail on the Mississippi after the 1993 flood, and I was just as-
tounded by how much devastation was caused by the controls that had been put
in place. . . . And so I started asking questions then: how could we do a better
job? And at that point and time, I was really good friends . . . with a fisheries
biologist that worked in North Carolina, and he kept saying "You know, there
is this guy named Dave Rosgen, and you really have to take his training." . . .
[When I finally was able to take a course from Rosgen in 1996] I was sitting there
listening to him, and I was thinking, "This is the answer! These are the clues that
I needed." . . . I sat there in that class, and it was sort of like a lightbulb coming
on, you know: these are the sorts of things that we need to consider to be able
to do a good job.[13]

Bledsoe and Greene were among the attendees at Rosgen's first North
Carolina course, and his emphasis on geomorphology really caught their attention. When Bledsoe moved to the state Division of Water Quality soon after-
ward, he helped channel funding from the Environmental Protection Agency's
section 319 program to sponsor the Rosgen courses at Pilot View (a nonprofit
Resource Conservation and Development Council discussed in more detail
below).[14] The explicit intention of the funding was to bring together in Rosgen's
short courses the various state and federal agencies starting to get involved in
stream restoration. As Bledsoe described it, "we funded that [the early NCD
courses at Pilot View] through a section 319 grant and paid for several agencies
to send staff. . . . The idea was to get a broad cross section of the state government agencies (and maybe a few federal) dealing with restoration of streams,
and get them all together in the same class."[15]

The early Rosgen courses at Pilot View created a community of restoration project managers and permitting staff who were in remarkable agreement
about how best to approach projects. Allan Walker, a veteran NRCS staff member, described that unanimity:

In North Carolina there were two or three people I know that were very interested in stream-type work that brought a lot of those ideas here: Dick Everhart,
Angela Greene/Jessup, and Joe Mickey that worked with NC Wildlife, and I became very interested right after they did. . . . Those were the folks that have attended a lot of the classes. But at the same time in North Carolina you had folks
with US Fish and Wildlife . . . with the Army Corps . . . folks with DWQ [North
Carolina Department of Water Quality]. Everybody kind of ended up being in
there [in the courses] together. It made for a real good relationship with everybody doing it together and keeping on board.[16]

This well-integrated group, who already had ties from their work on North Carolina's water quality programs, carried the torch of Natural Channel Design in the state. For example, Will Harman, at the time a North Carolina State University Cooperative Extension staff member (later a founding principal of Buck Engineering, one of the main restoration firms in the Southeast), learned about Rosgen's work from Angela Greene and another Natural Resources Conservation Service staff member, Dick Everhart, in what sounds like a remarkably collaborative process:

> [Angela Greene] and Dick Everhart, who is the other NRCS person, they had already started [taking Rosgen's courses], and so Angela would go and take . . . Level I, and we would kind of go out in the field together and play with all this stuff that she learned in Level I. And we developed this page of questions, and then I would go take Level I and ask all those questions. . . . [W]e did that all throughout . . . because Dave works in such a different setting than we work in, so we would find all these things, these issues and problems, and I could take those questions back.[17]

In addition to changing regulatory requirements to mitigate damage to streams and a cohesive agency community, another key factor in the adoption of NCD was educational support and community-building efforts by local institutions. The North Carolina State University Stream Restoration Program, part of the state agricultural extension program, offers short courses based on Natural Channel Design as well as running a biannual restoration conference that is the primary gathering for the restoration community in the Southeast.[18] And the Pilot View Resource Conservation and Development Council, the organizer and driving force behind the Rosgen short courses, really got NCD rolling in North Carolina in the mid- to late 1990s. Since then, Pilot View has effectively become the NCD mother ship in the South, organizing and hosting multiple Rosgen short courses in North Carolina every year since 1996 as well as sponsoring courses in Alabama, Florida, Georgia, Kentucky, Virginia, and West Virginia.

At this point, NCD is the defining characteristic of stream restoration in North Carolina. As Greg Jennings, professor at North Carolina State University and founder of the Stream Restoration Program, said, "I think everybody in the practice now is trying to create naturally stable channels . . . [using NCD approaches. Whereas] in the past, where people were focused on creating rigid, hard channels, at least in North Carolina now we don't have any regulatory flexibility about what we can create. If we're doing a stream restoration, it has to be a naturally stable functioning channel, because we can't armor a channel with concrete or rock and get a permit at this point except under very extreme circumstances."[19]

Like many states, North Carolina has multiple agencies that fund stream restoration. Five out of six of them explicitly require an NCD approach. Permitting agencies have an even higher level of preference for NCD: four out of five use NCD exclusively, and one uses it a good deal. Every single member of the stream restoration community in North Carolina that I interviewed had heard of Dave Rosgen, and all but two of them employed his approach in their restoration work. As David Phlegar, the water quality supervisor for the city of Greensboro, North Carolina, put it, "Rosgen's work and NCD are pretty much the standard here. If you talk about stream restoration that's the rule."[20]

When I asked members of the stream restoration community why they or their agency/organization had chosen to use NCD, the most common answers were because it was already in wide use, because it had positive environmental impacts on water quality and aquatic habitat, and because of permitting requirements (see table 3.1). When I asked about the strengths of Rosgen's work for their day-to-day needs, respondents' most common answer was that they used the NCD approach because it works (see table 3.2).

EXPLANATIONS FROM WITHIN THE FIELD

How did Rosgen rise to the top of the hierarchy in the stream restoration field in the United States over the space of a decade? Why were the knowledge claims he produced so readily and broadly adopted by consulting firms and local, state, and federal agencies as they were in North Carolina? This breadth and speed of adoption would be notable for any new set of knowledge claims,

Table 3.1. Reasons for adopting NCD	
Only game in town	6%
Communication tool	6%
Funding requirement	19%
Natural aesthetic	19%
Permitting requirement	31%
Positive environmental effects	31%
Everybody uses it	38%

Note: Respondents could list multiple reasons.

Table 3.2. Strengths of Rosgen's approach	
Communication tool	13%
No answer	19%
Natural aesthetic	25%
Quantifiable/predictive	38%
Positive environmental impact	50%
Stabilizes banks/it works	56%

Note: Respondents could list multiple strengths.

but it is really startling given the heated opposition of university- and agency-based scientists.

Having been stuck in the line of fire of the Rosgen Wars for more than fifteen years now, participants in the American stream restoration field have developed their own explanations for Rosgen's success. Both critics and supporters often point to Rosgen himself, particularly his field experience and his charisma. Rosgen is deeply knowledgeable about streams, with more than forty years of experience studying riparian systems. The depth of his field experience wins admiration even from some of his critics. As one US Forest Service staff member said, "Dave has walked as many miles of streams as anyone in the country. Natural Channel Design isn't coming from a guy sitting behind a desk. He's done it, gotten dirty, gotten his waders full of water like everyone else. That's very appealing."[21]

Rosgen is also a very charismatic man; people light up when they talk about him. He is the antithesis of a deskbound Washington, D.C., bureaucrat, an honest-to-god westerner from ranching stock who trains cutting horses and wears western shirts, a white cowboy hat, and an enormous belt buckle that he won in a cutting horse competition. He is energetic, opinionated, and extremely self-confident, and he speaks in practiced folksy phrases: idiots have "a terminal case of the dumb-shits," well-meaning idiots have "their heart to cranium ratio out of whack," and the actions of either kind of idiot are like "crapping your chaps and sitting in the saddle." As a US Forest Service staff member put it, "Don't underestimate the power of the individual behind this. He is mesmerizing. Kind of coarse, kind of crude, very funny. Doesn't give a rip what anyone thinks. . . . Dave Rosgen is as much an element of his success as his method. . . . You could have his method taught by some pencil-necked four-eyed academic, and it would go nowhere, but here's this . . . ass-kicking cowboy."[22]

Deep knowledge and charisma pack a potent punch, but they cannot stand as sufficient explanation for Rosgen's success because we have a strong counter-example: George Palmiter. Palmiter was another charismatic, self-trained, geomorphology-based, stream restoration consultant who rose to prominence at the same time as Rosgen in the late 1980s and early 1990s. Like Rosgen's, Palmiter's work was promoted in the 1992 NRC report on aquatic ecosystem restoration. And yet unlike NCD, Palmiter's approach was never widely adopted and he has faded from the scene. Thus while Rosgen's charisma and ability to read the landscape clearly contributed to his success, they are not sufficient to explain it.

Another common explanation within the stream restoration field is Rosgen's anointment by Luna Leopold. It is hard to think of anyone in the stream restoration world with more credibility than Leopold, who had tremendous scientific legitimacy (having been head of the US Geological Survey Water Division, a member of the National Academy of Sciences, and a recipient of the National Medal of Science) and was also widely revered among practitioners as the father of modern stream restoration in America. Leopold channeled that legitimacy into a serious effort to back Rosgen's play.

Leopold gave Rosgen a great deal of credibility by supporting his approach, coteaching his initial short courses, and writing the foreword to Rosgen's first textbook. Further, because of Leopold's eminence in the field, he was able to serve as a buffer between Rosgen and advocates of traditional hydraulic engineering until he established a base of support for his design approach. For example, a case study on one of Rosgen's early projects in the 1992 NRC report *Restoration of Aquatic Ecosystems* describes Leopold serving as arbiter between the US Army Corps of Engineers and Rosgen on the design of the Blanco River project, which "almost failed to materialize when COE [US Army Corps of Engineers] subjected the unique design to expert review and was told by its reviewers that the new system would not contain flood flows. The project design was then sent for review to Professor Luna Leopold at the University of California, Berkeley, Department of Geology and Geophysics; Leopold praised the project and expressed confidence that it would work. On the basis of his recommendation, COE withdrew its reservations, and the project was allowed to proceed" (National Research Council 1992, 474). Without Leopold's support, both supporters and opponents agree, Rosgen's work might never have achieved its current prominence. But at the same time, Leopold's endorsement was not sufficient, as it clearly failed to overcome the doubts of academically trained consultants and agency staff despite their admiration for him.

A third common explanation is that Rosgen used his decades of experience with the US Forest Service to develop an approach that met the bureaucratic needs of federal resource agencies, particularly in terms of time from project conception to completion. It is a truism in the public policy literature that bureaucracies prefer timelines that match easily with existing organizational structures, such as fiscal years. Thus the relatively speedy application of NCD is surely part of its appeal. But it is also important to remember that the stream restoration field is built on passion. Few, if any, restorationists would have picked up NCD if they were not convinced it worked. Thus while all three of these common explanations for Rosgen's success — his experience and charisma, the patronage of Luna Leopold, and NCD's correspondence with bureaucratic timelines — have some merit, they do not fully explain the widespread adoption and promotion of NCD.

There are also common reasons put forward by NCD supporters to explain the vehemence of their critics. The most common is professional jealousy. As John Potyondy, head of the US Forest Service Stream Team and Rosgen Wars moderate, said, "There's an element of jealousy [in their reactions to Dave] that no one will admit to over the fact that some cowboy from Montana was able to figure out how streams work and explain it to people."[23] Or as Gary Parker, a sediment transport researcher at the University of Illinois and Rosgen Wars moderate, put it,

> I think one of my colleagues hit the nail on the head when he argued that the un-derlying resentment on the part of academics had a lot to do with envy. Rosgen, by actually doing something and by developing at least some kind of a technique to do it, tapped into a market that was quite large, . . . for which there was quite a bit of enthusiasm, and which the academic community was not even trying to serve. Then Rosgen got all of this attention for it. . . . [The] surface expression . . . "Rosgen doesn't know what he's doing" had a subtext of envy: "Why is he getting all the attention? We're supposed to know more about this than him."[24]

Professional jealousy may indeed be a driver of the opposition, but it is not plausible as a complete explanation. Rosgen's critics, particularly in academia, have tenured jobs, scientific legitimacy, and prestige. Further, we must extend the same assumption of good intentions to academic- and agency-based scientists that we extended to agency staff above. NCD critics, too, care deeply about streams: if they believed someone had developed a restoration approach that worked, they'd likely be quite vocal in their support regardless of whether that person was sporting a doctorate or a cowboy hat.

There is, however, a second internal explanation for NCD critics' fierce and persistent criticism, this one provided by the critics themselves. They argue that Rosgen's classification system and design approach are flat-out wrong, wasting tax money and destroying streams. Federal agency scientist Daniel Levish expressed this sentiment when he argued that there are

> *huge* sums of federal dollars wasted on inappropriate "stream restoration." . . . When you consider that each of the people Rosgen trains applies his method to several hundred streams over their career, the potential environmental deg-radation is stupendous! These are things that can't be undone! So there's a huge amount of money that's been wasted, but there's also tremendous amounts of damage to stream systems, irreparable sorts of damage. . . . It's awful to watch people waste so much money and think they're doing good when they're doing harm.[25]

The next chapter assesses this claim.

CHAPTER FOUR

Capital Conflicts

> I'd like to make this sound simple, but it's not simple.
> It is doable, but you're going to have to spend a lot of
> time in the field, in measurement and observation.
> — DR. DAVID ROSGEN, Wildland Hydrology

The simplest question about Natural Channel Design turns out to be the hardest to answer: does it work or not? Despite the fact that NCD has been in use since the mid-1980s, there is shockingly little solid evidence with which to answer that question. Instead, we have decades of claims and counterclaims. Critics have repeatedly raised a whole slate of objections to which NCD supporters respond with their own broken-record set of refutations. Critics argue that use of the NCD approach actually harms streams, while supporters say they use Rosgen's restoration approach because it succeeds. They can't both be right. Yet the debate has persisted with great intensity and no visible change in content for almost two decades, like some demented scientific version of the movie *Groundhog Day*.

In this chapter I sort out the basic content of the debate. Because of the lack of definitive evidence, I draw on fluvial geomorphological theory, evaluations of restoration projects, and qualitative data to explain and assess NCD critics' and supporters' primary claims and to see whether we can in fact explain the vehemence of Rosgen's critics on purely substantive grounds.

THE SUBSTANCE OF THE ROSGEN WARS: CLAIM VERSUS COUNTERCLAIM

Rosgen's opponents raise an exhaustive list of concerns about Rosgen's classification system, design approach, recommended structures, and short courses as well as about his scientific practice and the scientific content of his work. This section attempts to explain and evaluate eight of the most common and substantive critiques.[1]

Despite the fact that claims and counterclaims about NCD have preoccupied the stream restoration community since the mid-1990s, there are remarkably few data available to resolve the substantive issues I will describe below. In the years since Rosgen first published his classification system in 1994, no one has mounted the kind of broad-based study of project outcomes that might be capable of resolving the debate. The complexity of fluvial systems and the high level of uncertainty of restoration science make the production of such conclusive data a considerable challenge. At the most basic level, it is not clear how researchers would establish equivalency between projects in different watersheds and hydrophysiographic provinces. Establishing comparability between practitioners is another thorny issue, given the wide variety of paths people travel to become successful restoration practitioners. Simply determining criteria for success is also complicated, given that for Rosgen and his supporters a successful project does not move, while for his opponents the goal is a dynamic channel. For all of these reasons a definitive, geographically broad, comparative study of restoration approaches would be difficult to carry out, but it is surprising that neither Rosgen nor his critics have attempted such a study, and only one paper has even suggested it (Juracek and Fitzpatrick 2003).[2]

Good case studies could provide useful, if not definitive, data. But here, too, we come up short. While critics have conducted powerful case studies of particular restoration projects (most notably, Soar 2000; Kondolf, Smeltzer, and Railsback 2001; and Smith and Prestegaard 2005), these studies have at best limited relevance, as the designers of the projects reviewed did not follow anything near the complete NCD approach.

Rosgen's supporters, for their part, have not conducted the type of detailed, published case studies necessary to meet scientific standards of evidence. Instead, they refute their critics with nearly twenty years of anecdotal evidence about NCD projects, typically claiming success rates of 80 percent and above.[3] Given that Rosgen's supporters are just as committed to healing riparian systems as their critics, their claims for project success should not be dismissed out of hand. Indeed, some of them are very convincing. For example, Buck Engineering (now a subsidiary of Michael Baker Corporation), a North Carolina firm with extensive experience implementing NCD projects, offers clients warranties on their projects that cover the costs of repairing or replacing any structure that moves for a set number of years after project completion. Those warranties are a *net source of revenue* for the company: once in place, the Rosgen structures Buck Engineering installs rarely move.[4] Still, the informal presentation of these and other claims limits their plausibility with Rosgen's critics.

Without data from broad comparative projects or even case studies, we have only geomorphological theory and, in some cases, social science data on NCD practice to draw on to evaluate the substantive claims and counterclaims raised by NCD critics and supporters. Where there is sufficient evidence to demonstrate that particular claims are fair or unfair I have done so, but some core issues remain unsettled.

1. Objections to Rosgen's Claims of Doability

Rosgen consistently argues that scientists have made restoration seem far more complicated than it is. In response, critics accuse him of empowering legions of undertrained enthusiasts with the confidence to get out the construction equipment and destroy streams in the name of helping them. As one federal agency scientist described it, "I think that was the biggest disservice that Rosgen did: he sold stream restoration as something that's simple. . . . [P]eople who were honest and educated realized that this was not a simple undertaking, and it might take years and lots of money to do correctly. And Rosgen came along and said . . . , 'Hey, it's really simple. Don't listen to them there scientists. Just do some stuff.'"[5]

While Rosgen certainly does emphasize doability, at no point in either the Level I or Level II course I observed did he describe restoration practice as simple or easy; quite the contrary, Rosgen consistently emphasized that restoration is difficult and requires experience. For example, at different points on the first day of the Level I course Rosgen had this to say:

> I want to caution you, sometimes I make things look a little simple, maybe because I talk fast. I hope you appreciate the fact that this is not simple. It takes another 280 hours of study at a minimum, and even then people have some difficulties because of lack of experience.

> I'd like to make this sound simple, but it is not simple. It is doable, but you're going to have spend a lot of time in the field, in measurement and observation.

It is crucial to emphasize, however, that for Rosgen "not simple" does not equal "uncertain," and it is here that Rosgen's critics have some traction. His overall message is clearly that with sufficient knowledge and training you can be confident that changes you make to a river system will perform the way you expect them to. As discussed in chapter 5, this leads to big differences in opinion between students in Rosgen's courses and students in rival short courses: based on my survey data, while 83 percent of Rosgen course respondents believed that restoration practice was more predictable than not, only 43 percent of students in an anti-NCD short course did.

Critics argue that the overconfidence produced by this mistaken emphasis on doability is deeply problematic because it encourages people without judgment or experience to intervene in, and thus damage, streams all over the United States in the name of restoration. Given the high degree of uncertainty about current restoration practice, Rosgen's critics' concerns about his emphasis on doability seem reasonable, but there is as yet no comprehensive data with which to evaluate whether this, in combination with the step-by-step NCD approach, produces greater numbers of project failures than non-NCD approaches.

2. Objections to the Exclusive Use of NCD

One of the most common objections that NCD opponents raise is that attending Rosgen's short courses is treated as necessary, and also as sufficient, by a growing number of agencies and municipalities (Gillilan 1996; Simon et al. 2007; Slate et al. 2007). Unless they have also taken Rosgen's courses, professors and full-time consultants with decades of experience cannot bid on projects. Critics argue that this exclusivity limits restoration practice by barring alternative approaches and experienced practitioners.

Karin Boyd, a consultant in Montana with twenty-five years of experience, including six years working for Stan Schumm, one of the most respected academic geomorphologists, said, "I definitely see RFPs [that require Rosgen training], and because I have not had Rosgen training [I don't bother applying for them]. You know it's kind of funny, those of us who've been doing this for some period of time, . . . Stan Schumm is a good example: he isn't going to go do Rosgen training, and so he can't go after those projects."[6] Scott Gillilan, a consultant with more than two decades of experience, simply abandoned public sector work because there are so many agencies that will "write into the RFP that you're going to do it this [Rosgen's] way. I've stopped trying to fight that battle, and I don't respond to those RFPs anymore. I got burned out trying to educate them [the agencies], and for the last five years, I've mostly been working for private clients."[7]

There is complete consensus among Rosgen's opponents and even moderates in the debate: the privileging of one method and one type of training over all others cannot stand. While agency-based decisions cannot be attributed directly to Rosgen, critics argue that he should use his authority to argue against such limitations. Rosgen's response to this criticism is not conciliatory. When I pointed out that agencies requiring NCD training bar even some practitioners he respects from restoration work, Rosgen had this to say:

That was a major surprise to me [when agencies began requiring my work]. My answer to that is that we have to listen to the message rather than shooting the messenger. The . . . reason that they're saying that is that consultants in the past responded to RFPs with more of the traditional [hydraulic engineering] work. And the states and agencies are tired of traditional work. The message is: we want to go to more NCD. What are universities teaching? Do you see universal teaching of NCD? No. . . . Here's my recommendation [for qualified practitioners excluded because they have not taken my courses]: go back and say, "Here's my qualifications towards NCD. . . ." Just because you've got a PhD doesn't mean you're qualified. All you got taught was traditional standard methods, . . . [and] what they're saying is they don't want to see any more of the traditional way we've been dealing with the rivers. I don't tell people I'm sorry. It's up to you to figure out how to give them what they want.[8]

Following Rosgen's advice turns out to be harder than he acknowledges, however. Despite the fact that they are not utilizing traditional engineering approaches to stream channels, bioengineering consulting firms such as Inter-Fluve and Milone & MacBroom report great difficulties convincing regulators who treat *Applied River Morphology* (Rosgen 1996) as gospel to accept alternative approaches that do not rely on NCD. As described above, many consultants have simply stopped trying and no longer respond to RFPs that require an NCD approach. Thus Rosgen's response seems insufficient. Although it is clear that he did not start this trend, it is within his power to soften it by encouraging agencies to be more open to non-NCD approaches that meet NCD goals of designing with nature.

3. Claims that NCD Infers Process from Form

A third common critique of NCD attacks the premise that it is possible to diagnose processes or predict channel response from an analysis of form (Kondolf 1995, 1998; Kondolf, Smeltzer, and Railsback 2001; Gillilan 1996; Juracek and Fitzpatrick 2003; Shields et al. 2003; Simon et al. 2007). Critics argue that what a channel reach looks like now does not tell you why it looks that way, and it certainly does not tell you where the channel is going next. As Kris Vyverberg, a geologist with the California Department of Fish and Game, put it, "People want to tell me it's a 'B' channel and then move on. I want people to describe it, tell me what's going on around the bend, why is it that way? . . . There is just a failure to realize that streams are more complex than can be accounted for by 'C3.'"[9]

A first step in evaluating this critique is to reflect it back at Rosgen's critics. When asked about their channel evaluation and design processes, every Rosgen critic I interviewed included key measurements of form. Long profiles, cross sections, and slope were universal objects of study, and without exception Rosgen's critics thought there was something to be learned from them about the processes at work in a reach. Andrew Simon, a researcher at the National Sedimentation Laboratory and passionate critic of NCD, wrote in a textbook on fluvial geomorphology methods that "channel form, or morphology, has long been recognized as a diagnostic tool in evaluating fluvial landforms. . . . The key to using channel form in the analysis of fluvial landforms must be based on either (1) measurements of parameters that aid in quantifying channel processes such as flow hydraulics, sediment transport, and bank stability or (2) *observations of diagnostic characteristics that provide information on active channel processes*" (Simon and Castro 2003, my emphasis). Clearly, Rosgen's critics consider channel form an important source of information about process. The issue thus becomes whether Rosgen's focus on form is as exclusive as his critics assert.

As demonstrated in the quote above, the two key processes critics typically point to are flows of water and sediment. Contrary to critics' assertions, the NCD approach does include measures of hydraulics and sediment transport. In fact, the entire ten-day Level III course is devoted to study of these processes, and many of the measurement techniques taught overlap with those of Rosgen's critics.[10] Clearly, the NCD approach does not simply infer process from form; Rosgen, like his critics, emphasizes both process and form. Instead, the crucial question is whether the *particular methods* for assessing flows of water and sediment incorporated into NCD are sufficient, and this cannot be assessed without a broad study of the outcomes of NCD projects.

4. Critiques of NCD's Insistence on Stability

A key sticking point for many of Rosgen's critics is his claims about channel stability (Kondolf, Smeltzer, and Railsback 2001; Juracek and Fitzpatrick 2003). This concern has two parts: (1) objections to NCD's foundational assumption that dynamic equilibrium is a common condition and an achievable restoration goal, and (2) a widespread perception that both Rosgen and his students go beyond dynamic equilibrium to favor "*stability* stability," channels that are not going to move no matter what flows hit them.

The first part of this objection — that NCD assumes the possibility of dynamic equilibrium — is an accurate description of Rosgen's position. In his lectures and writings, Rosgen continually puts forward stability as both the required characteristic of reference reaches and the desired outcome of restoration, and his definition of stability clearly corresponds to an idea of dynamic equilibrium: "the ability of a river, over time, in the present climate to transport the flows and sediment produced by its watershed in such a manner that the stream maintains its dimension, pattern and profile without either aggrading or degrading" (1994, 1996, 2007a).

This flies in the face of current scientific consensus. As Doug Shields of the National Sedimentation Laboratory argues, since the 1950s and 1960s, when the research on which Rosgen's work is based was published, geomorphology has moved toward "the idea that fluvial systems are inherently unstable. . . . [T]he idea of dynamic equilibrium is useful, but like an ideal gas it probably doesn't exist."[11] It also contradicts the field experience of consultants such as James MacBroom, who argues that the NCD approach is "based too much on the concept of the equilibrium channel, which is something we don't see very often. Most of our watersheds are very dynamic. We live in an urban area, so our watersheds are rapidly changing due to hydromodification of discharge, impervious cover, and storm drains, and also they have variable sediment loads."[12]

If Shields, MacBroom, and their colleagues are correct that dynamic equilibrium is the exception rather than the rule, then NCD projects should fail as soon as they experience flow of a magnitude sufficient to trigger adjustment of the reengineered channel. But despite the handful of widely publicized project failures cited by the NCD opposition, anecdotal evidence from Rosgen's students suggests that when they are implemented by experienced practitioners, most NCD projects stay in place, as demonstrated by the Buck Engineering warranty program.

It seems likely that the stability of these projects can be attributed to the second part of NCD opponents' concern: although Rosgen defines stability as dynamic equilibrium, in practice he and his students seem to favor channels that stay where they were put. According to Vyverberg, "There's a basic misunderstanding in the idea that here's where you put your meanders, here's where you put your bank revetments [and there they stay]. Meanders meander, but you're developing static control measures. . . . Rosgen folks are talking about *stability* stability: they're saying it's not going to change. . . . I can't speak to Dave's perspective on stability, but as the Rosgen Method is applied in the field, people seem to believe stability means the channel won't move."[13]

A preference for "*stability* stability" could explain why Rosgen's recommended restoration structures bear more resemblance to those of traditional hydraulic engineering than they do to stricter bioengineering approaches. Despite Rosgen's explicit insistence on dynamic equilibrium, the implicit message in the courses I observed was that properly designed and implemented channels do not move. He did not show slides of projects that adjusted from their initial form, nor did he ever discuss channel adjustments as a positive attribute of restoration projects. Further, the core techniques of NCD are not deformable: boulders and large pieces of wood tend to remain forlornly behind when channels migrate rather than moving with them.

Rosgen is beginning to espouse the use of some deformable techniques, but the lighter-impact bioengineering approaches are not in his textbooks, nor did they have any substantial presence in the Level I and II courses I observed.[14] All this sends a clear, if implicit, message to NCD students that the desired goal is stability. Even more than the insistence on dynamic equilibrium, the emphasis on stability directly contradicts the current scientific consensus, which emphasizes rivers as dynamic systems. Thus Rosgen's critics seem to be accurately describing the importance of stability for most NCD practitioners: the practice of hardening the channel to make it stable backs up the foundational concept of dynamic equilibrium.

5. Claims that NCD Does Not Pay Sufficient Attention to Biology and Ecology

A fifth common objection is that NCD is an inadequate guide for restoration because it does not address stream biology or ecology. Critics argue that because Rosgen is the only instructor in his short courses and lectures only on fluvial geomorphology and hydrology, he conveys to his students that they do not need to draw on any of the other disciplines to complete successful projects. NCD seems to be based on the assumption that if practitioners get the physical form of the channel right, the rest will follow; this is referred to as the "*Field of Dreams* hypothesis" (Palmer, Ambrose, and Poff 1997; Sudduth et al. 2011; Violin et al. 2011) or the "build it and they will come approach," with the "they" in this case being not a disgraced baseball team but fish, bugs, and ecological processes more generally.

In his short courses and writings, Rosgen occasionally mentions consulting with local "fish-squeezers" to get limiting factors analyses and other data relevant to his design process, but he never mentions a biologist collaborator the way he constantly references Luna Leopold and Lee Silvey, a geomorphologist and a hydrologist, respectively. While Rosgen does say in his courses that it is important to consult with other disciplines, critics argue that the solo practices of many of his students suggest that this message is getting lost along the way.

By contrast, NCD critics tend to stress that restoration is an inherently multi-disciplinary practice that depends on collaboration among geomorphologists, engineers, and biologists, among others. As engineer and consultant James MacBroom put it, "I think people need to be cross-trained and realize there's more to stream restoration than just the Rosgen technique. I think people need to be trained in the fundamentals of biology and stream ecology, because ultimately that should be the final product."[15] Critics' short courses reflect this, drawing in multiple instructors from a broad range of disciplines. In the academic short course I observed, for example, there were two primary instructors and no fewer than seven guest lecturers.

Whether you support the idea of a single cross-trained überrestorationist or a collaborative team of specialists, it is difficult to imagine restoration projects succeeding on multiple fronts without a concomitant range of expertise. Thus this critique seems fair: even if Rosgen wishes his students to work in multi-disciplinary collaborations, his solo teaching and restoration practice and the content he covers in his courses do not support that message.

6. Arguments that NCD Is Overreliant on Bankful Discharge

Perhaps the most common charge raised by critics is that the NCD approach is too dependent on the concept of bankful discharge. Many of Rosgen's critics see the centrality of the bankful concept as an irreparable fatal flaw at the heart of NCD (Juracek and Fitzpatrick 2003; Simon et al. 2007; Roper et al. 2008).

Bankful discharge has been variously defined (see Federal Interagency Stream Restoration Working Group 1998, 7.11, for a concise and useful overview), but the core concept is that, counterintuitively, the flow that shapes channel form is the result of small, fairly common storms, not the rare big storm (Wolman and Miller 1960). The relation between the frequency of flows and the magnitude of sediment they transport demonstrated in the Wolman and Miller paper is one of the most influential analyses in twentieth-century geomorphology and has thus drawn a number of follow-up studies over the last fifty years. There is widespread agreement that finding physical indicators of bankful discharge in the field can be very difficult (Williams 1978; Knighton 1984; Federal Interagency Stream Restoration Working Group 1998, 7.10–7.11). Beyond that, the current scientific consensus is that it is inappropriate to equate *bankful discharge* — the maximum flow a channel can sustain without spilling out onto the floodplain — with *dominant discharge* — the flow that determines channel form — because the relationship does not hold in arid and semiarid environments (Wolman and Gerson 1978) or in systems that have no flood-plains, are incised, or are currently adjusting to upstream influences (Doyle et al. 2007).

Critics are certainly correct that the bankful discharge concept is the key-stone of the NCD approach. Teaching students to find physical indicators of bankful discharge in the field was one of the primary foci of both the Level I and II courses I attended. It is critical to note, however, that *Rosgen's definition of bankful discharge is not tied directly to physical features of the channel itself*, as in the original Wolman and Miller paper and most of the work that followed it. Instead, following Dunne and Leopold (1978), Rosgen defines the bankful discharge as the dominant discharge: "The bankful stage corresponds to the discharge at which channel maintenance is the most effective, that is the discharge at which moving sediment, forming or removing bars, forming or changing bend and meanders, and generally doing work that results in the average morphologic characteristics of channels" (1996, 2–3). Further, by using regional curves, Rosgen can derive bankful discharge even in systems where physical indicators are misleading or absent. Critics' arrows thus fly wide of the mark when they critique the NCD approach based on conventional definitions of bankful flow.

7. Claims that NCD Is Overly Interventionist

Many members of the Rosgen opposition believe that we would be better off leaving the majority of damaged channels alone to heal themselves. To these critics, it does not matter whether the NCD approach is effective; the whole project of human intervention in rivers is flawed. For example, consultant Steve Gough said: "To me it's much better to leave a stream alone completely than to go in and manipulate it. And this [NCD] system is extremely biased towards getting out the yellow machines and rearranging the creek. . . . [V]ery very seldom in my experience is that what needs to be done."[16]

Gary Parker, a prominent sediment transport researcher and moderate in the Rosgen Wars, expressed this in less partisan terms: "My own view is that what I've seen tends to be in many cases too interventionist, and there has not been enough emphasis on how to encourage rivers to fix themselves."[17] Partly, this reluctance to intervene stems from the prevalent belief among NCD critics that restoration practice is highly uncertain, but part of it is also a sense that in many cases rivers are perfectly capable of healing themselves if we just get out of the way. As one federal agency scientist said, "Our primary recommendation in many cases was just set back the levees, widen the bridges, and leave it alone and you'll get it back eventually at lower cost, no maintenance, and not much monitoring. In anthropomorphic terms, the stream knows what to do."[18]

In an ideal world, this critique would be fair: we would leave all but the most threatened stream systems alone to heal themselves, and what restoration we did attempt would be done by local experts of great experience. What those who raise this objection overlook is the tremendous public demand and the regulatory requirements that have caused the stream restoration market to expand rapidly, hitting the billion-dollar-a-year mark in the mid-1990s and continuing to grow ever since (Bernhardt et al. 2005). Many in the stream restoration community, regardless of their stance on NCD, thus argue that we need some kind of guidelines or standards of restoration practice, even if they are ringed round with caveats and insistence on the specificity of local conditions.

If the *form* of the NCD guidelines is a necessary evil, then the issue becomes the *content* of the forty-step process, and here the jury is still out. Without a large-scale comparative study evaluating the success of projects that actually use the full NCD approach, there is no good way to adjudicate between claims from critics that NCD projects are inordinately prone to failure and claims from supporters that their current success rate is 80 percent or higher.

8. Critiques of Rosgen's Scientific Practice

Rosgen's critics in academia and the research branches of federal agencies care about restoration practice, but restoration *science* is their life's work, and many are outraged by what they see as Rosgen's departures from accepted scientific practice. Some critics begin at the most fundamental level, questioning Rosgen's lack of academic credentials. They point out that he has little formal training in the subject he teaches, that his recently granted PhD required no course work, which is not unusual for British PhDs, and that it was completed under the supervision of a person who at the time was effectively Rosgen's employee, Dr. Richard Hey.[19] "Why does he have to teach in this workshop format if he's so legit?" remarked a US Forest Service employee with academic training in geomorphology who was forced to attend a Rosgen course by her supervisor. Or, as a federal agency scientist put it, "What I don't understand is without any . . . real training or background or anything else, how does he get written into the regulations?"[20]

The most central critique of Rosgen's scientific practice, however, focuses on his refusal to comply with the norms of peer review: he often does not indicate the number of data points or the geographic locations from which the data were collected on his graphs, he does not publish in peer-reviewed journals, and he does not make the data sets on which his knowledge claims and proprietary models are based available for review. To Rosgen's critics, this is not simply a clash of cultures or a failure to pay respect to sacred cows. In their view, the way that science progresses is through communication and critique. By failing to provide access to the data supporting his work and to participate in the peer-review system, Rosgen opts out of the project of scientific progress in the eyes of his critics.[21]

What seems clear is that although Rosgen follows some academic forms, he is fundamentally a consultant operating under the constraints of the market, not a scientist paid to produce peer-reviewed articles. Thus critics' claims that Rosgen does not follow the norms of peer review are accurate; the question is how much that refusal matters. It clearly slows evaluation of his work considerably and discomfits many of his critics, but if his design approach and models are proven to work consistently, this departure from conventional scientific practice may not be particularly important.

NCD PRACTITIONERS' COUNTERCLAIMS

While Rosgen is clearly frustrated by the constant barrage of critique, he for the most part demonstrates considerable poise under fire, meeting his critics' barbs with grace and good cheer. He could not be described as taking those barbs lying down, however, as he and his supporters constantly push back. The following sections evaluate the counterclaims that NCD proponents put forward.

1. Counterclaims that NCD Is Not the Enemy

NCD supporters tend to view the US Army Corps of Engineers through the lens of righteous wrath and see themselves as David to the Corps's Goliath. Despite the fact that the Natural Channel Design community and the Corps share the goal of creating stable channels, Rosgen and his supporters consider the Corps a clear and present danger. They are thus perplexed and frustrated by their critics' attention, which appears to them as pointless infighting when the real enemy is lurking nearby, concrete at the ready. This raises two questions: Are critics as uninterested in the US Army Corps of Engineers as NCD supporters claim? Is the Corps still a serious threat to American rivers and streams?

The answer to the first question is clearly yes. To Rosgen's critics, the Corps is no longer the primary enemy. None of the critics I interviewed mentioned the Corps as a current threat to riparian health. For them, the bête noire is indeed Natural Channel Design, not one of the three federal agencies that, over the last hundred years, did so much of the damage restorationists are trying to undo (the others being the Natural Resources Conservation Service and the Bureau of Reclamation).

The answer to the second question is more complicated. The flood-control work of the US Army Corps of Engineers during the twentieth century radically changed the flow of surface water across the United States. If the Corps had chosen the path of least hydraulic resistance and controlled flood damage by moving people and infrastructure out of the floodplain, the American riparian landscape would look much different than it does today. But the steady expansion of the Corps's role had more to do with protecting existing property and investments than with preventing flood damage per se (O'Neill 2006). The primary instruments of flood control were not designed to synchronize the patterns of human development with the rhythms of the river but to force rivers to move in conformity with the beat of agrarian capital and urbanization. Channelization and levees, concrete and riprap: these were the tools and techniques that became, over the course of the twentieth century, the pillars of hydraulic and civil engineering practice in this country.

The result is a riparian landscape of startling sterility, with profound human interventions in systems large and small: creeks you can cross in a single stride have been culverted or lined in concrete all over this country, and engineering works on our major rivers have fundamentally transformed them. The extent to which the interventions of the US Army Corps of Engineers and hydraulic engineering more broadly are likely to remain on the landscape is an open question; many sources suggest that the days of these ubiquitous works of public engineering are numbered (among them the engineers who built them).[22] But they are here now, the dams and the levees, the conveyance channels and the concrete-lined settling ponds, and they have sparked a great deal of outrage. Thus the Corps has long been a boogeyman to the restoration community: while too large to fit in anyone's closet, the concrete-lined ecological desert the Corps made of the Los Angeles River still serves admirably as nightmare.

Nightmares of the US Army Corps of Engineers, however, should probably come with a time stamp. Implementation of the National Environmental Policy Act in the early 1970s made it far more difficult to carry out large, federally financed channelization projects, and the 1986 Flood Control Act actually made restoration part of the mission of the Corps. Of course, this did not mean that the entire organization tossed out the concrete and embraced a new day: the dozens of districts of the Corps have a high level of autonomy, and each has taken up the new mission with differing levels of enthusiasm, or lack thereof. But the Corps is now in the river restoration business itself, most famously in

Florida, where it is busy putting back into the Kissimmee River many of the bends it carefully removed just forty years earlier.

Further, the US Army Corps of Engineers is a key source of guidance documents and standards of practice for sediment control and hydraulic engineering. The Corps's Hydrologic Engineering Center develops technical documents and software packages that are widely used by restoration scientists and practitioners, including some of Rosgen's students. The Corps's Engineer Research and Development Center is another important source of technical information and instruction for the broader restoration community, again including those who utilize Rosgen's approach.

Thus although the change in mission for the Corps is still very much a work in progress, NCD supporters' objection that critics are ignoring the primary threat to riparian health is probably not fair. On the other hand, as should be clear from the section above, there is as yet no definitive evidence that NCD is a worthy target of critics' wrath either.

2. Assertions that Critics Have No Practical Experience and Thus No Standing

A second common counterclaim raised by Rosgen and his supporters is that objections to NCD, particularly those from university-based scientists, are worthless because critics have no constructive suggestions to replace what they attempt to discredit. John Potyondy, program manager for the US Forest Service Stream Systems Technology Center and a moderate in the Rosgen Wars, put it this way: "Academics lament that people don't come to them. Maybe they understand rivers, but they haven't been able to communicate that to people with needs. And they don't have the experience. It's easy to be critical of failed projects, but they can't say, in most cases, 'This is what I've done.'"[23]

Rosgen often phrases it in ways less directly critical of academia, but it is the same message. For example, during the Level I course I attended, Rosgen said, "There's a rule, you guys: if you criticize someone else's restoration project, you better be able to explain what went wrong and give them some advice about how to fix it. . . . You can't come along and just be the critic; you've got to say what they should have done." Or as he put it in a paper he presented at the 2006 American Society of Civil Engineers conference in Omaha: "Surprisingly, the most vocal critics also have the least experience in conducting river restoration" (Rosgen 2006, 10).

As a description of Rosgen's opponents, this critique falls somewhat flat. It is true that a number of the most vocal NCD critics are researchers who seldom if ever design restoration projects themselves. But it should be obvious from all the quotes from consultants in the sections above that many critics are themselves restoration practitioners who regularly design and implement projects.

Where this counterclaim has more traction is on the lack of concrete alternatives. While any non-NCD practitioner would happily suggest alternative approaches for a particular project, critics have not developed an alternative step-by-step design approach to take the place of NCD because their insistence on the complexity and particularity of stream systems makes such a universally applicable system seem ludicrous. Thus in terms of general design guidelines, the counterclaim has some merit: NCD critics have not, and may not ever, offer a comparable set of design guidelines for restoration practice.

3. Claims that Critics' Objections Are Based on Naïveté

In response to objections that NCD is overly interventionist (critique number 7), Rosgen and his supporters argue that critics are closing their eyes to reality: refraining from action is a luxury we rarely have, given our habit of building on floodplains. Rosgen's most common example of this is not threatened bridges or other major infrastructure but more simply a farmer about to lose his barn: "I've got some guy standing on the bank with his barn about to fall in the river saying, 'Hey, what can you do to help me?' I'm gonna have to make a decision. It may be the wrong decision, but you have to do *something*. You don't have the luxury of saying, 'Let me study this for ten years.' You've gotta make some calls."[24]

Similarly, Rosgen argues that his critics are naive when they accuse him of empowering legions of undertrained students to overconfident restoration practice (critique number 1). As he pointed out during one of our conversations, a large proportion of the students who show up for his Level I course are *already* designing restoration projects: "I always ask how many people are already doing restoration in the first class [Level I], and over half the hands go up.[25] Am I responsible for these people? If I can help them, I will. Their bosses have already forced them to fix rivers. They're taking this training because it's what's available."[26] Thus Rosgen argues that accusing him of egging on unprepared students with claims of doability is specious: they are actively engaged in restoration before they set foot in his first course.

The first of these counterclaims — that calls for noninterventionist responses are naive — has some merit. As I discussed above, in an ideal world we would leave rivers and streams alone to heal themselves, but there are serious regulatory and economic forces promoting intervention: federal and state water quality rules require us to address sediment from eroding banks and channels, and we continue to treat land areas devastated by floods as nature's gift of cheap land for new waterfront development.[27]

The second of these counterclaims — that Rosgen is not empowering but instead attempting to educate legions of undertrained students — is more complicated. Although a substantial minority of Rosgen's opponents feels that he should be held no more responsible for his students' failures than university professors should be for their students', the majority of the opposition argues that as their sole educator and enabler, his students' actions are his fault. At first glance it seems hypocritical to nail the failures of Rosgen's students to his door without attributing similar levels of responsibility to university professors. But very few professors actually teach restoration courses. Even those who do teach restoration-related university classes or short courses often address narrowly defined issues, such as sediment transport, rather than the broader training available in Rosgen's courses. Thus there is some rationale for holding him more responsible for his students' work than, say, a professor teaching Introduction to Fluvial Geomorphology. Further, students walk away from short courses taught by Rosgen's academic critics with a clear sense that neither they nor anyone else really knows how to do restoration; this caution stands in stark contrast to the confidence of practitioners who have attended Rosgen's courses (see chapter 5 for a more detailed discussion). Thus while it is not appropriate to hold Rosgen primarily responsible for the actions of people who take one or two Rosgen courses and think that is all they need, the counterclaim does not completely undermine the initial critique.

4. Claims that Critics' Objections Are Based on Ignorance

A final way that Rosgen and his supporters directly counter critics' arguments is to point out that most critics do not know enough about NCD to have a solid basis for critique (e.g., Rosgen 2006, 10). In reflective moments, some of his critics acknowledge this as well: *none of Rosgen's major critics have attended his short courses*, the primary way in which information about the NCD approach is disseminated.[28] Because of this, several of the primary critiques of Rosgen and his work are based on misapprehensions of what he actually practices and teaches. Two directly address the abridged list of critiques above.

While it is true that the bankful discharge concept is the keystone of the NCD approach, NCD practitioners do not measure it the way critics think they do (see critique number 6). Rosgen teaches his students to determine bankful elevation using data from regional curves; the physical indicators of bankful discharge that critics correctly assert can be absent or misleading serve only as a preliminary guide for NCD practitioners, not the determining factor, as some papers critical of the classification system have assumed (e.g., Juracek and Fitzpatrick 2003; Doyle et al. 2007; Roper et al. 2008). Similarly, while it is true that Rosgen's approach works largely from data on channel form (critique number 3), it also employs a number of process-based components that opponents overlook rather than engaging with constructive critique; for example, the entire ten-day Level III course is devoted to the study of sediment transport and hydraulics. Thus in this case NCD supporters are correct: as these two powerful examples demonstrate, critics are ignorant of some key features of what Rosgen actually teaches.

CRITIQUE AS MOBILIZATION OF CAPITAL

The review of claims and counterclaims in the previous two sections highlighted some important but deeply perplexing characteristics of the Rosgen Wars. First, some of each side's key claims are obviously incorrect. Just as NCD supporters' assertion that their critics have no hands-on experience or practical skills ignores the large number of practitioners in the anti-NCD camp, critics' claim that the keystone of Rosgen's system (bankful discharge) is fatally flawed turns out to be based on misapprehension of what he actually teaches. Second, there is no evidence to resolve a number of the most central claims and counterclaims. Most fundamentally, *we do not know whether* NCD *works.* This makes the tenacious opposition to NCD's spread even more notable, because if there is one thing academic and agency scientists do not have, it is free time. Why would NCD critics put so much effort into a crusade they have no definitive evidence is needed? Finally, it is important to note that the claims and counterclaims described above have been mobilized in essentially the same form since the mid-1990s without anyone bothering to gather the data to resolve them.

This last characteristic of the debate, in particular, suggests that there is more going on than a fight over how water should run through dirt. *If some of the central assertions in the Rosgen Wars are groundless, most are unresolved, and all have been repeated unchanged for nearly two decades, something other than their content must be at stake!* Bourdieu's concept of capital and the role it plays in scientific debate can provide a useful beachhead for explaining this perplexing state of affairs.

Bourdieu most commonly uses capital in a nonmonetary sense. He argues that capital is not a fixed object that keeps its character regardless of the field in which it is mobilized but instead an active *social power relation specific to a particular field* (Bourdieu 1996b, 264). The species of capital that are valued in a given field both enable those who hold them to succeed and define the character of the field itself. For example, a first author publication in *Science* or being principal investigator on a large National Science Foundation grant carries a great deal of capital within academia but is essentially worthless in the fine arts or professional sports. Capital is thus both a weapon and a stake in struggles for power and "allows its possessors to wield a power, an influence, and thus to *exist*, in the field under consideration, instead of being considered a negligible quantity" (Bourdieu and Wacquant 1992, 98–99).

Using capital as a currency that is neither static nor secure but instead in constant need of assertion against competing claims, we can reframe the debates described above as dueling attempts to capture resources in a zero-sum game. The substantive issues in the fight over Rosgen's work are important, but just as important are the mobilization and defense of claims to capital and thus status and authority.

1. Species of Capital

The grounds on which participants in the Rosgen Wars base their assertions of scientific expertise and authority are diverse and often defined in implicit opposition to their opponents: the ability to produce practical tools versus the capacity to generate theoretical understanding; the mastery of hands-on experience versus the possession of scientific credentials; the ability to control versus the acknowledgment of complexity; the exposed but righteous stance of the maverick versus the shelter of the scientific community. These are all claims to authority, and thus types of capital, mobilized in the Rosgen Wars.

Mobilizing them can be a surprisingly difficult task in the stream restoration field. There is no national conference on stream restoration, nor is there a journal that serves as clearinghouse for the field. Dave Montgomery, professor of geomorphology at the University of Washington and armchair Rosgen critic, described the problem of reaching his target audience:

> Say someone in my position decided they wanted to engage in a big debate about Rosgen: where would you go, how would you engage? Would you send Dave a nasty letter? That's not my style. Comment on one of his papers? Others are doing that. Most of the people that really need to hear what you could cast as a debate are not equipped to adjudicate it: they're wanting knowledge. There's no outlet for communicating directly with them except through a short course. So it's not clear what the choices are for framing that debate.[29]

In response to these complications, members of the NCD opposition use a variety of arenas to try to make their case. As Andrew Simon, a prominent NCD critic, describes it, he and his colleagues "decided we need to keep publishing in journals, but a lot of these people [Rosgen's supporters] don't read journals, they just go home with their handbooks. So we also have to teach short courses at national technical meetings, and teach classes at federal agencies to reeducate, or reindoctrinate them. And we have to engage all the time at these meetings and continually pump papers in. The problem is that we have to educate not just the people on the ground but their bosses and their bosses' bosses."[30]

To the three arenas to which Simon points — peer-reviewed journal articles, conference presentations, and short courses — I would add two: attempts to establish national guidelines for restoration practice and to develop national-level restoration curricula. The entrance requirements for each of these arenas and the forms of communication they enable are quite different: the types of arguments that can be made (and thus the species of capital that can be mobilized) in the loosely structured format of a five-day short course are quite different from those in the tight confines of a fifteen-page peer-reviewed article, as are the species of capital required to participate in them in the first place.

For example, authors of peer-reviewed articles typically need to demonstrate that they hold particular types of capital valued in the basic science field: compliance with the norms of scientific practice, highly developed analytical skills, and mastery of the currently accepted knowledge base particular to a given field. Yet the scientific strengths of peer-reviewed articles can make them poor tools for convincing NCD supporters that they have boarded the wrong boat and are sailing off into dragon-infested waters: articles' typically quite neutral tone discourages powerful rhetoric, and getting past peer-review gatekeepers often requires a level of analytical sophistication that makes the details of an argument inaccessible to many NCD supporters.

By contrast, conference presentations, particularly at technical (as opposed to academic) meetings, do not require the scientific capital produced by association with prestigious institutions for participation. While their shorter length limits the complexity of the analysis that can be presented and thus the scientific capital that can be wielded, it also makes conference papers far more accessible, not to mention allowing considerably more room for rhetorical hardball. And in fact conference organizers have encouraged participants to pour gasoline on the fire. As one conference organizer said, "I've put on two international conferences . . . , and in both instances I set [the Rosgen Wars] up as one of the sideshows, like a circus. Watch everybody fight over whether

Dave walks on water or has horns coming out of his head. 'Cause it's either one or the other."[31]

Where do Rosgen and his supporters mobilize their arguments? Certainly not in the peer-reviewed literature. Very few of Rosgen's supporters have sufficient scientific capital and knowledge to conduct the types of research accepted in peer-reviewed journals, analyze and present their data in a standard academic format, and drum up the financial resources to support research, analysis, and writing. This presumes that they wish to publish in the peer-reviewed literature in the first place. It is important to remember that publications are the currency of universities and federal research agencies; Rosgen and his supporters typically have other sources of capital. Even if NCD supporters decided to engage in academic journals, they would face peer-review boards that are often quite hostile to their approach. Thus Rosgen and his supporters have focused their efforts to persuade others of the importance of the types of capital they hold on the range of arenas that are more open to them: conference proceedings papers, short courses, and self-published textbooks.

2. Capital in Practice

The NCD opposition's basic tactic has been to insist that the types of capital that matter in stream restoration should be the same as in basic science fields: credentials from prestigious institutions, compliance with the norms of scientific practice, ability to abstract theoretical principles from empirical data (as in the development of models), and correspondence with the current scientific consensus. According to NCD critics, Rosgen, his work, and his supporters do not possess these types of capital and thus should not be considered authoritative or even legitimate parts of the stream restoration field.

In practice, critics make these points in many different ways in the arenas discussed above. For example, in a 2005 conference paper (Simon et al. 2005), some of Rosgen's most vocal critics mustered multiple assertions of the importance of scientific capital and Rosgen's lack thereof on every page. The opening salvo insists that Rosgen's approach is scientifically bankrupt, describing NCD as a pseudoscience based on outdated work that was irrelevant to restoration design even in its heyday: "The para-professional training provided by some involved in 'natural channel design' empower[s] individuals and groups with limited backgrounds in stream and watershed sciences to engineer wholesale re-patterning of stream reaches using 50-year old technology that was never intended for engineering design" (Simon et al. 2005, 1).[32] This same paper ends with a ringing assertion of the centrality of scientific practice, knowledge, and legitimacy as the authors aim and fire the established scientific "canon" at NCD:

> The foremost advantage of the process-based approach is that it is well established in the scientific and engineering literature. For decades, geomorphologists and hydraulic engineers have been quantifying river processes and developing models that have been tested and refined over time. Developing a design using this rich literature leverages off of a substantial scientific background, and thus provides a critical foundation from which to defend the design approach. Such literature and historical precedence is lacking for the classification approach. Practitioners concerned with professional liability and with the future of their professions would do well to provide design services based on peer-reviewed professional standards. (Simon et al. 2005, 10)

A less inflammatory but no less assertive statement of the centrality of scientific capital in the stream restoration field comes from a 2006 attempt by the National Center for Earth-surface Dynamics (NCED) (the host of the conference described in the preface) to establish a national stream restoration curriculum.[33] While the center has deliberately avoided taking a stance in the Rosgen Wars, the proposed curriculum topics practiced critique via exclusion, clearly indicating that Natural Channel Design would be no more than a minor implement in the restoration toolbox envisioned by the authors — a nail-set rather than a hammer. Tellingly, the intended implementers of the proposed curriculum were universities, an attempt to move the center of disciplinary reproduction back into academia and away from the private sector. The premise that the university should occupy a central position not only as the primary trainer of practitioners but also as the main developer of new knowledge and applications is a clear assertion of the importance of basic science capital.

NCD supporters respond to these mobilizations by insisting that the key types of capital defining success in the stream restoration field should not be the computer and white coat of the lab scientist but the rite-in-the-rain field notebook and mud-coated waders of the experienced riverhand and field scientist. They assert the importance of practical solutions to human problems such as flooding and bank erosion, accessibility to a broad audience, hands-on experience, and correspondence with nature as opposed to traditional hydraulic engineering.

For example, at a 2006 conference Rosgen simultaneously asserted his own capital and debunked that of his critics when he argued that practical application is the highest value in stream restoration and that his critics clearly lack it because they focus on critique rather than applicable knowledge: "To the author's best knowledge, no available analytical or process-based models predict the depth and slope for runs and glides, transverse bar features, point bar slope, and other features of riffle/pool stream types such as a c4. . . . Unfortunately, critics do not offer alternate design strategies that would improve the current state of the science of river restoration implementation" (2006, 4–5).

An example of Rosgen asserting another type of scientific capital comes from the introduction to his most recent textbook, *Watershed Assessment of River Stability and Sediment Supply* (WARSSS). Rosgen emphasizes his connection to Luna Leopold and asserts his scientific credentials by referring to himself as a *teacher of scientists*: the intended audience for the WARSSS method is consistently described as "scientists" by both Rosgen and the EPA, which commissioned Rosgen to develop the WARSSS approach (Rosgen 2007b).

Finally, Rosgen promotes the capital stemming from working with natural processes and environmentalism — environmental capital — in his short courses by taking on traditional hydraulic engineering and even goes so far as to identify his critics as old school engineers rather than as the actual cross-cutting coalition of academics, agency staff, and practitioners who make up the NCD opposition. For example, in the Level I course I observed, Rosgen implied that his methods were excluded from textbooks because they were not traditional engineering methods, rather than the actual situation: academia, the most common source of textbook authors, is a hotbed of anti-NCD sentiment: "The geomorphic solution, the Natural Channel Design method, you're not going to find in a model, you're not going to find in a lot of textbooks. . . . We have to get away from our traditional river engineering approach, which is still in the textbooks. Right now, the better option is not in the book."

Reviewing the merits of the claims and counterclaims in play in the Rosgen Wars demonstrates that the substantive and political contents of the Rosgen Wars are deeply intertwined. When critics object to NCD on the substantive grounds that it promotes stable channels and thus flies in the face of the current scientific emphasis on channel dynamism, they are also asserting the importance of the types of scientific capital they hold and claiming that the types Rosgen holds are inferior. When Rosgen and his supporters argue that critics do not know enough about NCD to critique it, they also assert that critics are violating the norms of scientific practice and thus possess less scientific capital than they claim. And when NCD supporters argue that critics should take on the US Army Corps of Engineers rather than fellow restorationists, they are simultaneously asserting that it is they who hold environmental capital, not their opponents. The substance and politics of the Rosgen Wars are, in Bourdieu's phrasing, two translations of the same sentence: *the fight over content is the fight over capital.*

CONCLUSION

In this chapter I investigated whether one side or the other in the Rosgen Wars was obviously correct so that we could explain their vehemence and persistence on substantive grounds. But the substantive core of the Rosgen Wars cannot explain them: the same claims and counterclaims have been in circulation, largely unchanged, since the mid-1990s, and while each side makes some plausible claims, others are unsupported by definitive evidence or just plain wrong.

This is not an analytical failure but the foundation of all that follows. There would be little intellectual interest in the Rosgen Wars if it were simply and self-evidently the case, as supporters claim, that NCD was the best thing since sliced bread. The opposition could be safely consigned to the category of sour grapes, and everyone could go on about their business. Conversely, if, as critics claim, NCD could be definitively proved false, its supporters could be explained away as part of the venerable American tradition of devoting ourselves to the teachings of charismatic snake oil salesmen. The careful analysis of the claims and counterclaims at the heart of the Rosgen Wars in the first sections of this chapter shows that neither of these scenarios is a plausible description of what is happening in the American stream restoration field.

Instead, the seemingly irresolvable character of the debate is an unmistakable indication that the Rosgen Wars are more than a fight over restoration methodology. Bourdieu's concept of capital suggests that the Rosgen Wars are simultaneously a substantive argument and a fierce battle over scientific legitimacy with winner-takes-all stakes. The internal power structure of the stream restoration field is on the line.

This is a clear explanatory advance over where we stood at the beginning of the chapter, but it raises an immediate question: how did Rosgen and his supporters gain enough capital to go head-to-head with the consecrated forces of scientific legitimacy? How did they garner a sufficient base of support to challenge academia, and why are they winning the fight? To answer those questions, we need to analyze the practices of participants in the stream restoration field and the ways those practices have been shaped by Rosgen and his work.

CHAPTER FIVE

Building a Base of Support

> Once I went to that first short course, it just clicked in my head
> that *this* was what I was looking for: a quantifiable system that was
> repeatable . . . [and] that was based on nature. And that was it.
> — CHERYL HARRELSON, principal, Steady Stream Hydrology

In the previous chapter we explored the intellectual substance of the Rosgen Wars. The inescapable conclusion was that while substantive questions are central to the Rosgen Wars, so too are power struggles over what kinds of capital should have primacy in the restoration field. The existence of the Rosgen Wars begs a more fundamental question, however: how did Rosgen manage to build a base of support strong enough to allow him to challenge the elite of the restoration field in the first place? Part of the answer lies in the day-to-day practices of the participants and institutions that make up the field: the training, tools, and standards of practice that enable the restoration field to function. Thus this chapter focuses on basic questions of social practice in the restoration field. How does someone become a participant in the stream restoration field? Why do the majority choose to get their training from Rosgen rather than from a university? How has Natural Channel Design become the de facto standard of restoration practice in the United States?

UNIVERSITIES AND THE (MIS)EDUCATION OF RESTORATION FIELD PARTICIPANTS

Let's say you want to join the stream restoration field. How would you get the training you need? You might think a university would be the place to go, but it turns out to be surprisingly difficult to get stream restoration training within the American university system. No university in this country has a department of stream restoration. There are some state and polytechnic universities that offer concentrations in stream restoration as part of degrees in other subjects, such as environmental or watershed management. As described in chapter 3, North Carolina State University offers restoration training through its agricultural extension program (rather than through conventional course work). There are also three universities (Portland State University, the University of Minnesota, and the University of Washington) that have restoration certificate programs. But it is not yet possible to get an academic degree in stream restoration in the United States. At best, people interested in stream restoration can attempt to cobble together a suite of reasonably relevant courses in ecology, geomorphology, hydrology, and/or engineering from the existing course offerings at their university. Nobody, including the students themselves, thinks this is adequate.

The absence of academic training and certification is a serious issue in the stream restoration field. There are certainly professions where no university training is expected or needed (carpentry, aesthetics, farming, etc.), but stream restoration is an environmental *science*, and in the sciences the traditional source of training is the university. Even in fields with a strong industry presence in knowledge production, such as biotechnology and the petroleum industry, the university is the main training ground for practitioners. Thus the fact that academia has been slow to respond with programs focused on restoration science or practice makes it difficult to gain the knowledge needed to participate in the field and to tell who within the field knows enough to be a competent designer, manager, or regulator.

There has been high demand for trained restoration practitioners for more than two decades. Why have universities so far been unable to develop the programs needed to educate and certify the needed restoration workforce? Based on my interviews with academics who tried to start such programs, there seem to be four basic reasons. First, the disciplinary structure typical of American universities creates some technical difficulties. Although interdisciplinary programs are very much in vogue at present, the vast majority of degree programs are still organized along disciplinary lines. Fulfilling the requirements of her home department typically makes it quite difficult for a student seeking a BS or MS degree to take the range of courses necessary to prepare her for work in the very interdisciplinary field of stream restoration. While MS students often have more flexibility, they are more limited in terms of available courses because they are only enrolled for one or two years. But even a PhD program may not have the necessary interdisciplinary scope. Steve Gough, a restoration consultant in Missouri, tried to put together such a course of study for his PhD at the University of Illinois and was rebuffed: "I started fishing around, and the walls between academic departments are just still very strong. I had a professor tell me that at the U of I you're either going to be a geomorphologist, or you're going to be a fish biologist, or you're going to be a civil engineer, but you're not going to be even two of those things, let alone three; you're going to be one. That's all you can be in today's academic world."[1]

Second, there are not many universities where the range of course work necessary for training in stream restoration is already in place. There are a few centers of restoration science (such as Colorado State University, the University of Minnesota, and the University of Washington) where the broad range of necessary knowledge is already available from existing course offerings. It is likely no accident that two of the three existing certificate programs are at schools on that list. Most universities do not have this luxury and thus would have to develop a suite of new courses to start a restoration program.

Another reason why existing university-based education has not been sufficient to meet the training needs of the field is that what many would-be practitioners require is *retraining*: they already have bachelor's degrees and have neither the need nor the desire to return to college. PhD programs are both too narrowly focused and too time intensive for midcareer professionals with mortgages and families. Even master's degree programs are a stretch for this core body of would-be practitioners, particularly given existing programs' limited ability to provide a targeted restoration education. As Laura Wildman (at the time of our interview a senior staff member at American Rivers, the most prominent river-focused NGO in the United States) described the situation, there are very limited options:

> I have a strong interest in fluvial geomorphology, and I'd like to continue to educate myself. Who has a class in fluvial geomorphology? Very few universities in this country. How do I take it? I live in Connecticut. And yet I really want to take a bunch of high-level courses from a professor. So I go to Yale to the geology department, where there's one fluvial geomorphology postdoc, who doesn't teach. The postdoc's supervising professor is more focused on his one particular topic of research and seems unconcerned with how I learn about this in the future. Do I want to be a PhD student and work on his very specific project that has nothing to do with restoration? No. And guess what: everywhere I go it would be like that. Now there are a few universities with fluvial geomorphologists interested in restoration, but I can't move out there, and do I really want to be a PhD student anyway? I'm applied. I've always been applied. I love applied. So . . . I've reached some bizarre roadblock where no one cares about teaching me. I want to be better, I really want to train myself in this. My one door available is to give up my career for six or seven years and do a PhD.[2]

A fourth reason why universities have not served their traditional role as educators and certifiers of competence is that becoming an adequate restoration practitioner requires a major component of learning by doing. Although this is less true of many state schools, research universities do not typically encourage apprenticeship as part of degree requirements. Nor do faculty at research universities typically have the extensive hands-on project experience to be able to provide such field training. So even if a university was willing to include an apprenticeship component in a degree program, it would likely have to turn outside its tenure-track faculty to implement it.

The only attempt I know of to start a hands-on restoration practice course for students at a research university was spearheaded by Ann Riley, one of the most prominent restoration practitioners in the country. She tried to start an apprenticeship program through her nonprofit to serve students at the University of California, Berkeley, and the University of California, Davis, but it only lasted one semester because of lack of support from the universities. When asked about the (in)adequacy of current academic training, Riley had this to say:

> Right now the universities are light-years behind what the practitioners are do-ing. There's no place for anyone to go to school to learn this stuff. . . . So people like Dave [Rosgen] and I, we're reduced to holding these *workshops* and trying to pull in as many people as possible. The answer is to have apprenticeships. People should get training at the universities, but the professors are not practitioners and don't know how to do that kind of training. You need to have nonprofits or pro-fessional schools or something like that where people can go to learn on the job.[3]

Despite the difficulties of starting new programs, during the 2000s four universities (Portland State University, the University of Minnesota, the University of Washington, and West Virginia University) successfully developed restoration certification programs. While West Virginia University's program no longer exists, the University of Minnesota and Portland State University programs (both launched in 2006) and the University of Washington program (begun in 2010) appear to be going strong.

These programs may be an indication that universities are trying to move into their typical niche, but as of yet the certificate programs are too small and too new to have had a significant impact on the restoration field. Since the mid-1980s, when the field began its current expansion, most would-be restoration practitioners have been unable to find the programs they needed via the traditional university pathway. Instead, they have turned to restoration short courses, primarily those taught by Rosgen.

RESTORATION SHORT COURSES

Given the widespread adoption of Rosgen's classification system and Natural Channel Design approach in the United States, it is notable that with only a few exceptions you cannot study his approach at a university. Most academic fluvial geomorphology courses do a brief review of the Rosgen classification system as part of an overview of a number of classification systems — Montgomery and Buffington, Schumm, Whiting, etc. — but you wouldn't need to take off both shoes to count the universities that teach students to apply the classification system, and you can count the programs that teach Rosgen's design approach on one hand.[4] And yet Rosgen's is the most widely *learned* restoration approach in this country because he has been extraordinarily successful at circulating and disseminating his work through short courses.

Short courses are a common form of education in environmental science fields. Short courses typically focus on a narrowly defined topic, last anywhere from a few hours to a few days, enroll somewhere between twenty and forty students, and include some mix of classroom and field time. Sometimes short courses are offered as continuing education for professionals; sometimes they augment established degree programs. The stream restoration field is unusual in that short courses are its primary form of training, not a supplement to university-based degrees.

Since Rosgen offered his first short course in 1986, he has taught almost 14,000 students. To give some sense of his schedule, in 1995 he taught 534 students in 13 courses lasting 65 days; in 2011 he taught 605 students in 14 courses lasting 88 days. It is important to note that these numbers only include the courses that were open to the public; they do not count the courses arranged by agencies or organizations exclusively for their staff, which increase the student count by an average of 8 percent each year.[5]

Rosgen's short courses have evolved dramatically. In the late 1980s there was just one course, and it typically lasted only a few days. There are now six courses, each of which lasts five to ten days.[6] The core short courses are arranged into four levels (which do not map onto the four levels of the classification system). Level I, Applied Fluvial Geomorphology, is a five-day course that introduces students to the classification system, field methods, and basic theory of fluvial geomorphology, sediment transport, hydraulics, and restoration. Level II, River Morphology and Applications, is a five-day course that focuses on application of Rosgen's classification system and reference reach approach. The ten-day Level III course, River Assessment and Monitoring, goes beyond the earlier courses' focus on form to delve into the processes that determine that form, studying erosion, sediment transport, and the influence of riparian vegetation. Finally, the ten-day Level IV course, River Restoration and Natural Channel Design, provides the tools for assessing, designing, and implementing restoration projects. Each of these courses is the prerequisite for the one that follows. Complete all four and you are considered to be Rosgen certified, which requires a minimum commitment of thirty days of course work and $7,400, not counting either transportation time and costs or the cost of room and board during the courses themselves.

According to Wildland Hydrology, Rosgen's consulting firm, approximately 61 percent of students stop at Level I, 17 percent stop at Level II, 8 percent stop at Level III, and 13 percent go all the way through Level IV. This steep tapering off is not surprising given that many of the people who take Rosgen's course are regulators or managers; they need to get the overview but will never need to classify a stream themselves, much less design a restoration project.

There are alternative short courses. Some are organized by Rosgen critics in academia, federal research agencies, or consulting firms. Other courses are offered by more neutral parties, such as the US Army Corps of Engineers' Engineer Research and Development Center. The only regularly offered, well-known series of courses that provides an alternative to NCD, however, is the two-level short course series developed by a loose-knit group of academics including Matt Kondolf, a geomorphologist at the University of California, Berkeley; Margaret Palmer, an aquatic ecologist at the University of Maryland; Jack Schmidt, a geomorphologist at Utah State; and Peter Wilcock, a sediment transport researcher at Johns Hopkins. I refer to these courses in the remainder of the chapter as the "academic short courses." I will say more about the differences between the academic short courses and Rosgen's below, but for now it is worth noting that the academic short courses are both much newer than Rosgen's and reach fewer than one-fifth the number of students each year.

At this point, approximately two-thirds of the American restoration community has taken one or more of Dave Rosgen's short courses.[7] And it is through these short courses that we begin to get a glimpse of how deeply Rosgen has shaped the day-to-day practice of participants in the stream restoration field. To explore these practices and their effects on the stream restoration field, I use Bourdieu's concept of habitus.

THE SHORT COURSES AS SHAPERS OF PRACTICE

Habitus is one of Bourdieu's foundational concepts, and it is central to his explanations of social reproduction: the ways in which particular practices, class structures, and so on reproduce themselves over time. Habitus describes a set of embodied dispositions, learned through some form of educational institution, which do not govern behavior but do make particular actions likely. Every field has its own habitus that shapes and defines the practices within it.

In his article on the specificity of the scientific field, Bourdieu says that scientific habitus consists of the "systems of generative schemes of perception, appreciation and action, produced by a specific form of educative action, which make possible the choice of objects, the solution of problems, and the evaluation of solutions" (1975, 30). In other words, participants in a field are profoundly mentally and somatically shaped by the education required to participate in that field. The intellectual and physical training they receive shapes their perception and understanding of the systems they study, the questions they ask about those systems, and the kinds of solutions they find good. Linked by these shared frameworks of conscious and subconscious behavior and understanding, the uncoordinated actions of the myriad participants in a field create a coherent set of patterns and outcomes, which Bourdieu refers to as the *subjective structure* of the field.

If Rosgen's short courses were sufficient to create a habitus and thus a subjective structure for the stream restoration field, that would go a long way toward explaining the strength and breadth of his support. But are the NCD short courses habitus producing? As many observers on both sides of the debate have wryly noted, Rosgen's courses have certainly produced a large group of people who want to *be* Dave Rosgen and a strong sense of community among participants, but does this have the intellectual and somatic reach of habitus?[8] To answer this question, I compare the organization, materials, and student pools in Rosgen's short courses with their most serious competition: the two-level academic short course discussed above.

Short Course Organization: "A specific form of educative action"

Short courses differ from the course work typically required for a professional qualification such as a master's degree in a number of key ways that shape the educational experience of their students. The amount of material that can be covered in a short course, even the five-day or longer courses that Rosgen and his critics teach, is substantially smaller than in a university course. Thus the range of information presented in short courses is necessarily much narrower than that included in a traditional university education, although that narrow focus means that the material covered is far more precisely targeted for relevance to stream restoration.

Because short courses compress a great deal of content into a very brief period, students have little time to reflect on the material presented, ask questions, and attempt to put it to use. Trying to absorb the content presented in short courses has more in common with attempting to drink from a fire hose than from the more measured cup of university courses. Thus students often report that they come out of a short course thinking they generally understood the material and then discover substantial holes in their understanding when they try to apply what they thought they had learned. These students cannot sign up for office hours or ask questions in lecture or lab the following week. Their only recourse is going to additional short courses.

Finally, short courses differ from the standard university structure in creating a total immersion experience, far from family, work, or other instructors who might question the premises being taught. They thus have the capacity to create intellectual conversion experiences despite their short time scale. Angela Greene, an engineer with the Natural Resources Conservation Service, described attending her first Rosgen course in 1995 and thinking, "This was the answer! These were the clues I needed . . . [and] the sorts of things we needed to consider to be able to do a good job."[9] Restoration consultant Cheryl Harrelson described a similar aha moment when she attended her first Rosgen course: "Once I went to that first short course, it just clicked in my head that *this* was what I was looking for: a quantifiable system that was repeatable . . . [and] that was based on nature. And that was it."[10]

All three of these characteristics — the targeted material, the overwhelming flow of information, and the absence of contrasting opinions — are typical of restoration short courses, but there are also distinctive aspects of Rosgen's courses and students that do much to create a habitus and thus a unified subjective structure for the stream restoration field. Rosgen's courses are distinguished from the academic short course series by an intense focus on teamwork. Based on a field experience survey all students must complete before the course begins, Rosgen divides course participants into four teams that form the basis for all of the fieldwork and in-class exercises during the five to ten days of the course. On field days these teams survey, sketch, and sweat together as they gather data on their assigned reach of stream; at night they gather at big tables, subsisting on take-out food and lukewarm coffee over the long hours it takes to convert their field data into the spreadsheets and graphs required for Rosgen channel classification and design. Connections among teammates are even more firmly cemented by the communal presentation and critique of those spreadsheets and graphs the next morning, an educational hazing experience that is the source of considerable bonding even among those who took Rosgen's courses at different times.

By contrast, in the academic short course that I observed, team-oriented work played a very limited role despite the emphasis on restoration as a team endeavor. While students were divided into groups for field exercises (three students to do the long profile, three students for cross sections, etc.), these groupings were spontaneous and not built into the organization of the course. Other assignments were completed individually.

There are also notable differences between the take-home materials distributed in Rosgen's courses and in the academic short course I observed. These materials are critical because they become the primary resource for students once the course is over. In Rosgen's courses the take-home materials seek to emphasize the legitimacy of the information presented. They include a bound, tabbed course notebook with background material and detailed instructions for the field exercises and, most importantly, a copy of one of Rosgen's textbooks.[11] This is a far cry from the ad hoc handouts in the academic short course, which provided students with a far greater range of information but left it up to each individual to explore it.[12]

There are also take-home gifts from the Rosgen courses that allow graduates to advertise their membership in the NCD camp. (In)famously, those gifts used to include a T-shirt that read, "If you don't know bankful, you don't know shit!," cheerfully including short course students in the cowboy culture of the NCD community. Because so many of the students in Rosgen's courses worked at federal agencies, however, which are not allowed to fund such profanity, the T-shirts were regretfully phased out. Still, even the new tamer gifts — in Level I a Wildland Hydrology ceramic mug, in Level II a Wildland Hydrology commuter mug and tape measure, and in both a signed certificate of completion — allow Rosgen students to advertise the fact that they have been through the courses and to identify others who have been, too.

Another key difference between the Rosgen and academic courses is the students they attract. Rosgen and his critics draw from the same pool of potential students: primarily midcareer agency staff and consulting firm employees moving into the stream restoration field. Based on data from a survey I conducted of short course students, the introductory Rosgen and academic short courses seem to be attracting different sets of students from that shared pool. Most notably, the educational levels and exposure to science and engineering curricula appear to be lower among Rosgen's students. (These data must be considered indicative rather than definitive, as the response rate to my surveys was only 50

Table 5.1. Highest level of educational attainment by short course participants

COURSE	ROSGEN LEVEL I	PERCENT OF TOTAL	INITIAL ACADEMIC	PERCENT OF TOTAL
High School	1	4.3	0	0
BS				
life sciences*	3	13	2	16.7
physical sciences†	3	13	0	0
engineering	0	0	0	0
other‡	0	0	0	0
MS				
life sciences	4	17.4	2	16.7
physical sciences	6	26.1	3	25
engineering	0	0	4	33.3
other	4	17.4	0	0
PhD				
life sciences	1	4.3	1	8.3
physical sciences	1	4.3	0	0
engineering	0	0	0	0
other	0	0	0	0
TOTAL	23	100	12	100

* ecology, chemistry, wildlife management

† hydrology, geology, forestry

‡ humanities, social sciences, public administration, law

percent for the Rosgen course and just 44 percent for the non-Rosgen course, twenty-three and twelve respondents, respectively. The full text of the survey is included in section C of the appendix.)

As shown in table 5.1, the respondents from the academic short course had on average attained higher levels of formal education than those in the Rosgen course: while just under 17 percent of the respondents in the academic short course had stopped with bachelor's degrees, 26 percent of Rosgen's students had stopped at that level, and one had only a high school diploma. (I know from talking to students in the Rosgen Level I course that there were at least

Table 5.2. Current roles in restoration

	DESIGNER	FUNDER/ REGULATOR	PROJECT MANAGER	OTHER*
Rosgen Level I	30%	26%	43%	48%
Initial academic	42%	25%	58%	33%

* operator, habitat assessor, surveyor, monitor, educator

four people with only high school diplomas in attendance, but the other three did not respond to the survey.) Further, while 58 percent of the respondents from the academic short course had a background in the physical sciences or engineering, only 43 percent of Rosgen's Level I students did (none in engineering). Fully 17 percent of the respondents from Rosgen's course had no science background at all. Rosgen's students thus seem to bring a relatively lower level of familiarity with accepted scientific material and practice and are that much more open to developing a restoration habitus based on Rosgen and his teachings.

The idea that Rosgen's students are likely to be substantially more open to taking on his stream restoration habitus is supported by other survey data as well. Students in the academic short courses bring with them more experience designing and managing restoration projects (table 5.2), suggesting that the initial academic course may be used to fill in specific aspects of restoration — geomorphology and sediment transport — for people who are already familiar with the field, whereas the Rosgen Level I course is used as an introduction to stream restoration in general. Supporting this, only one respondent from the academic short course said that they took it in order to learn more about stream restoration in general, whereas almost half of the Rosgen course respondents did (table 5.3).

The data in table 5.3 also demonstrate that the NCD approach is firmly embedded in the practice of many agencies and consulting firms. In response to an open-ended question about why they chose the course they attended, more than a third of respondents from the Rosgen course said they were there because their employer or workplace required it; no one attended the academic course for this reason. Further, a quarter of Rosgen course respondents said that they were there because Natural Channel Design was so widely accepted and/or well known; none of the respondents from the academic course mentioned the instructors' design approaches.

Table 5.3. Reasons for selecting/goals for particular short courses

REASON / GOAL	INITIAL ACADEMIC	PERCENT	ROSGEN LEVEL I	PERCENT
Required by supervisor / workplace	0	0	8	35
Recommended by coworker or supervisor	4	33	3	13
Learn about geomorphology / hydrology / sediment transport	11	92	5	22
Learn more about restoration in general	1	8	11	48
Alternative to Rosgen	3	25	0	0
Learn Rosgen's classification and / or approach	0	0	11	48
Reputation of instructor(s)	5	42	3	13
Widely accepted / well-known method	0	0	6	26

Note: Respondents could list multiple reasons or goals.

Short Course Content: "[W]hich make[s] possible the choice of objects, the solution of problems, and the evaluation of solutions"

Rosgen's short courses clearly constitute a "specific form of educative action," in Bourdieu's terms, but to inculcate habitus they must have distinctive content that ensures that course graduates will focus on a particular set of problems, solutions, and evaluative criteria. Further, the content must go beyond the conscious to reach the level of ingrained, subconscious action. Do Rosgen's short courses in fact do this?

At first glance, the answer would appear to be no. Despite the fact that the academic short courses were set up in critical response to Rosgen's, there is a good deal of overlap among the materials they present. Both the initial academic course and the Rosgen Level I course critique traditional hydraulic engineering and introduce the basics of hydrology and fluvial geomorphology, upon which they agree up through the early 1960s. Further, the basic survey techniques taught during the field days on the two courses are nearly identical.

In both courses, students are taught to do long profiles and cross sections, and, although they disagree about the breakpoint between the active channel and the banks, the core method for selecting and sorting sediment particles is identical. Several of the biology-trained restoration practitioners I interviewed said that they could not differentiate between the material presented in the Rosgen course and early versions of the initial academic short course; even some of the handouts were identical. Thus one immediate objection to the claim that Rosgen's short courses produce a distinctive habitus would be that the content he teaches is too close to the content of the academic short courses to constitute a distinctive set of claims and practices. There are, however, clear differences in the questions asked, solutions proposed, and overall level of certainty of outcome in the two sets of courses.

First, the two sets of short courses ask quite different questions and focus on different measurements to answer them. For example, as described in chapter 2, the fundamental starting point of NCD is regional curves: empirical data on regionally typical relations between the size of a drainage basin and the discharge, cross-sectional area, and bankful channel width of streams within it. Because regional curves are so critical to the NCD approach, Rosgen-trained practitioners put a great deal of effort into collecting regional curve data, often working collaboratively with other NCD practitioners in their area to produce them. By contrast, the non-NCD restoration practitioners I interviewed said they considered the hydraulic geometry relations produced by regional curves only late in the process (if at all) as one of multiple checks on the reasonability of proposed designs.[13] For NCD practitioners, the regional curves are foundational, the nonnegotiable starting point of analysis. Non-NCD practitioners, by contrast, start with questions about flows of water and sediment and the basin-wide history of channel movement and land use.

A second key difference is the role of channel classification in problem analysis. The first step in any NCD analysis of a stream potentially in need of restoration is to classify the channel. By contrast, non-NCD practitioners not only avoid the Rosgen classification system unless forced to use it by clients but, if left to their own devices, do not use *any* type of classification system as part of their evaluation process. This difference is important in two ways. It means that NCD practitioners expend a good deal of energy collecting data on morphological features that are not considered in academic practice, such as bankful and flood-prone width. More critically, eschewing classification means that academically trained practitioners typically start with a system's unique qualities, whereas NCD practitioners start from its similarities to other systems. This is a profound difference.

The design process provides a third example of the distinct content emphasized in Rosgen's short courses. For NCD practitioners, designing a new channel form depends on the availability of reference reaches: regionally identified stable stream reaches of the same classification within the same valley type. Reference reaches allow NCD practitioners to set ranges for sinuosity, depth, and other key design parameters. Reference reaches are also a critical tool for many non-NCD practitioners, but they identify and use reference reaches in different ways that depend on assessment of geology and flows of water and sediment rather than Rosgen's channel or valley classifications (which address those factors indirectly). Non-NCD practitioners also tend to look for one or two directly comparable pristine reaches of the same scale rather than a range of reaches that may be impacted by human activity as long as they are stable, as in NCD.

Perhaps the most important difference between the content of the Rosgen and academic short courses, however, is that while the latter cover a wide range of fields in a somewhat scattershot fashion, the former present a specified, comprehensive system of knowledge claims — Rosgen's classification system and design guidelines — that are purportedly applicable to any stream, of any size, anywhere. The universal, systematized content of Rosgen's courses thus provides the categories of perception, appreciation, and action central to habitus. *The form of the knowledge claims Rosgen produces is central to his ability to circulate them.*

Further, these knowledge claims are consistently presented as certain; for Rosgen, restoration is a doable project. When asked about the level of uncertainty associated with restoration practice, Rosgen had this to say: "I have a great degree of certainty in the designs *if* you get them built right. That's the biggest weak link that I see in this business. And that's where most people fall apart. . . . When I see that done right I have great confidence. . . . I haven't been doing this for forty-seven years and thinking we're taking a shot in the dark. That's one of the strengths that I can stand up on, because I can take you to hundreds of rivers that have responded the way we predicted."[14] By contrast, the fundamental uncertainty of current restoration science and practice was the main take-home message of the academic short course, reiterated multiple times a day.

In the survey of students from the Level I Rosgen course and the first academic short course, I asked the following question: "Based on the information presented in the course, how predictable or unpredictable do you think restoration work is?" I asked respondents to circle a number on a scale from one to ten, where one was totally unpredictable and ten was totally predict-

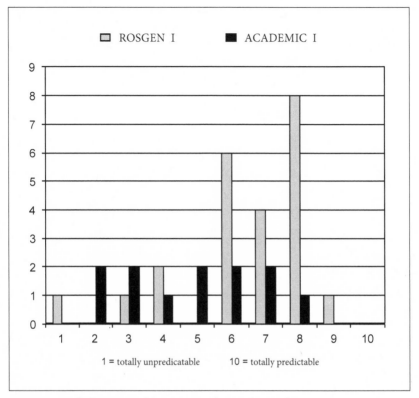

Figure 5.1 Level of certainty of restoration work according to short course participants.

able. Despite the fact that a substantial portion of the students in each course came in with some hands-on experience with restoration projects and thus could be expected to hold views on the relative certainty of restoration practice independent of what the instructors taught, there were still clearly visible differences between the two groups of respondents (figure 5.1). The average level of certainty posited by Rosgen course respondents was 6.5 out of 10, almost 2 points higher than the 4.8 posited by academic course respondents. Even more tellingly, while 83 percent of Rosgen course respondents believed that restoration practice was more predictable than not, only 43 percent of academic short course students did. At a very basic level, the Rosgen short courses encourage participants to view stream restoration as an already viable practice. By contrast, the academic short courses encourage participants to view the current practice of stream restoration as a crapshoot, overstepping the limitations of the science.

The discussion above concerns the explicit content of the short courses, but habitus is not only based on systematized, comprehensive beliefs; those beliefs must be *internalized* to the point of becoming embodied practices that make particular actions very likely. Rosgen's short courses create these embodied habits through intensive fieldwork components that train participants physically in the actions needed to apply the classification system and NCD approach. Over the four levels of courses, the movements associated with Rosgen's approach — the particular actions required to perform surveys of channel form, determine bankful elevation, and assess typical sediment loads — become deeply ingrained, so that *the way in which Rosgen's knowledge claims are circulated is integrally related to their intended application.* These embodied practices are often reinforced when students return to their places of work: almost 50 percent of the Rosgen students who responded to my survey reported that they attended the short course because it was required (35 percent) or recommended (13 percent) in their office.

I would thus argue that the answer to the question posed above — can Rosgen's short courses inculcate habitus in a Bourdieusian sense — is yes. The intensity and lack of alternatives characteristic of the short course format in general means that these courses can have an educative impact far out of proportion with their length, and Rosgen's courses are organized to concentrate that impact through intensive teamwork. Although provisional, my survey data suggest that Rosgen's students are less likely to come in with a developed scientific or restoration practice habitus, thus making them more open to adopting Rosgen's. Further, nearly half of the students were there because they came from a workplace where NCD is standard practice, suggesting that for many students, dispositions acquired during the short courses would be reinforced after leaving them. Finally, the problems identified and solutions proposed in Rosgen's courses are distinct from those in the academic short courses, and they are presented in a comprehensive, specified, certain system that reaches the partially subconscious, ingrained level of habitus through constantly repeated actions.

Rosgen's short courses are indeed "a specific form of educative action, which make possible the choice of objects, the solution of problems, and the evaluation of solutions" (Bourdieu 1975, 30), and they are central to the development of stream restoration habitus. Further, the ways in which Rosgen circulates his knowledge claims are deeply linked to the production and application of those claims, integrating research, training, and practice into a coherent whole. His short courses have thus been steadily populating consulting firms and regulatory agencies throughout the United States with people whose restoration habitus was shaped by Rosgen and his design approach.

BECOMING THE STANDARD OF PRACTICE

The sections above describe what happens once a student arrives at a Rosgen course, but why do students end up there in so much greater numbers than in the academic or other short courses? Writing in 2011, it looks like a simple question of availability: although there is minor fluctuation, Rosgen typically teaches fifteen courses per year with forty available seats in each (and long waiting lists that ensure every seat is full), reaching 600 students each year; the two levels of academic short courses are offered a total of four times per year to a smaller audience, 110 students in 2007.[15] There are more than five times as many opportunities to take a Rosgen course.

In the early 1990s, when the short course market took off, however, Rosgen taught far fewer courses, and there were a number of other options. Why did Rosgen's courses, classification system, and design approach become the standard? I argue in this section that the key reason was their correspondence with the needs of resource and regulatory agency staff and of consultants. In effect, the form of Rosgen's knowledge claims and the way he circulated them enabled their application in day-to-day practices and thus allowed the field to function.

Rosgen's Classification System as Lingua Franca

Stream restoration requires coordinated efforts among members of a number of different disciplines, such as biologists, ecologists, engineers, hydrologists, and geomorphologists; even if designers come from only one discipline, as is often the case in small consulting firms, the regulators who must sign off on the project typically come from a broader range of fields. Yet biology- and physics-based disciplines have quite different training, which causes confusion over even very basic things, such as which bank of the river is left and which is right: geomorphologists reference right and left off the flow of water and sediment downstream; fisheries biologists reference off the upstream movement of anadromous fish.

Communication is thus a significant hurdle: if differently trained experts cannot agree on a description of the current character of the system they wish to modify or even on which of its elements are most important for system health, how can they design its future form (Montgomery 2000)? Vaughan Voller, a civil engineering professor at the University of Minnesota and a principal investigator at the National Center for Earth-surface Dynamics, described the problem as follows: "The nomenclature is really critical. You've got to be talking about the same thing. You often have long discussion and debates with ecologists, which is an extremely descriptive science, talking to an engineer, which is extremely quantitative. And sometimes it's very difficult to bridge that gap, because you think you're talking about the same thing, but you're not; you're arguing about something that basically boils down to semantics."[16]

Rosgen's (1994, 1996) alphanumeric classification system fills this gap, creating a shared terminology that allows practitioners to communicate effectively and quickly grasp the key morphological characteristics of a stream system. Underlining this point, Syd Brown from the California Department of Parks and Recreation pointed out: "Hydrologists speak very well to hydrologists, engineers speak very well to engineers. What I think Dave did was transcend those . . . very real vocabulary barriers and provide a way for people to actually have a common understanding and a common language."[17]

Beyond *disciplinary* boundaries, the Rosgen classification system is also intended to transcend *geographic* boundaries, providing a universally applicable framework for describing streams for the American stream restoration field as a whole. Tim Keane, a professor of landscape architecture at Kansas State University and staunch Rosgen supporter, described the classification system this way: "It allows communication, because people know what you're talking about when you're talking about a c4 no matter where you're at."[18]

The Rosgen classification system is thus widely used, or at least understood, even by people who would not dream of using the other components of Rosgen's design approach. As Dave Montgomery, professor of geomorphology at the University of Washington, pithily put it: "The great strength is that it's a convenient shorthand, and at that level it's brilliant, and I really mean that. It's simple, and it's elegant. In terms of shortcomings, you know, it's kind of like, where do you start?"[19]

By providing the lingua franca for the restoration field, the Rosgen classification system has become a key element of restoration habitus, helping to produce the "systems of generative schemes of perception, appreciation and action" (1975, 30) that Bourdieu argues are a key component of habitus. The common language also sets NCD apart from other restoration approaches and allows initiates to recognize each other with ease. Fluency in Rosgen's classification systems is an important source of capital among Rosgen's supporters.

Design Guidelines as Standards of Practice

In addition to his classification system, Rosgen (2007a) has developed the only set of purportedly universally applicable methods for channel reconstruction projects. There is no competing methodological framework being put forward by academics because their insistence on the complexity of stream systems makes the idea of a universally applicable system appear ridiculous. Because of liability issues the engineering community has started to develop rival guidelines, but this initiative is only just getting under way and is unlikely to produce solid results for years. For the present and near future, at least, the NCD approach provides the only solid footing of specified standards of practice for restoration practitioners and thus helps produce the common actions that are another critical component of habitus.

The design guidelines have obvious utility for practitioners, but they are perhaps even more critical to the functioning of the *resource and regulatory agencies*. There is a large group of agency staff at the local, state, and federal levels who have been confronted with the Sisyphean task of choosing consultants, managing contracts, reviewing projects, issuing permits, and writing legislation to produce successful stream restoration projects. These staffers are the ones charged with reconciling our deeply contradictory goals for stream restoration: the return of nature and the simultaneous extension of human control. Agency staff are thus central to the daily practice of stream restoration. But how are they to evaluate the differences and decide between a proposal prepared by an academically trained fluvial geomorphologist and one prepared by an NCD practitioner? And perhaps even more importantly, on what basis can they justify that decision to their superiors and the public at large and thus avoid lawsuits?

Bill Heatherman, the stormwater engineer for the city of Overland Park, Kansas, described the quandary he faced in an e-mail to the American Society of Civil Engineers' River Restoration Committee:

> One reason why regulatory agencies may be so inclined to require Rosgen courses is because of the lack of credentialing (so far) or even consistent academic course work sequence that one could use to screen out people who should have some skills at design-scale stream geomorphology and those that clearly don't. This is not to say Rosgen's course is an adequate, acceptable, or optimal training program — only that it's the only one readily advertised and easily recognizable as such.
>
> [In 1999, as] a City official without a strong background in the discipline . . .

but a desire to see our streams managed better, I first gravitated to Rosgen because his work was so noticeable in the "Interagency Stream Manual" and because he offered a short course in our region. Before long, I was able to realize the limitations of his approach, and by the time we tried to begin putting things in practice, we had already widened our perspectives quite a bit. It was difficult, though, to justify why we accepted the work of some consultants in geomorphology, but not everyone who came knocking on the door. (Heatherman 2005)

How can the decision to accept the work of some consultants and not others be justified? Content seems the obvious ground for distinguishing between the approaches, but there is sufficient overlap between Rosgen and his critics that it requires a substantial knowledge base to see the differences, much less to understand why they matter.[20] Experience could be another possible justification for accepting one camp of consultants over the other, but there are very experienced practitioners in both.

What remains, then, is the bureaucrat's safe haven of justifiability: the application of accepted standards (Bowker and Star 1999; Espeland 1998; Porter 1995). The only set of standards, spelled out step by step, against which it is possible to check a channel reconfiguration design is Rosgen's; even if a regulator or resource manager does not herself have the ability to run that check, she knows that it is in theory possible to do so. Thus the fact that NCD provides standards of practice is critical to its utility for the field.

Agency staff, in return, have played an enormous role in promoting Rosgen's claims to scientific expertise. As discussed in chapter 2, agency staff at the local, state, and federal levels are the anchors of the NCD community, and federal agencies such as the Environmental Protection Agency and the Natural Resources Conservation Service have provided critical support for Rosgen by insisting that the knowledge he produces be learned and applied and by commissioning him to develop national standards and protocols. Resource and regulatory agencies powerfully support Rosgen's claims to legitimacy and expert status.

Short Courses as a Key Source of Educational Capital

The NCD design guidelines are critical for the stream restoration field because they provide standards of practice that consultants can employ and that agency staff can wield as justificatory shields. Rosgen plays another key role in enabling the day-to-day practice of the restoration field as a provider of educational capital, which is critical not only for creating competence in the field but also for creating *perceptions* of competence. Bourdieu writes: "Competence [is] a *social authority* which legitimates itself by presenting itself as pure technical reason. . . . In reality, the august array of insignia adorning persons of 'capacity' and 'competence' . . . the academic distinctions and scientific qualifications of modern researchers . . . modifies social perception of strictly technical capacity" (1975, 20).

As discussed in the initial section of this chapter, universities have not stepped into their typical role as the primary training ground for practitioners and the gatekeeper of legitimate qualification. This poses a substantial challenge to the stream restoration field. Without university degrees to provide educational capital in the form of a widely recognized credential, stream restoration consultants have struggled to establish their legitimacy.

The Rosgen short course series fills this gap, creating a system for disseminating knowledge of the NCD approach that offers a broadly recognized source of educational capital: on their résumés, consultants list prominently the level of Rosgen courses they've completed, and many firms state on their websites that they have staff who have completed Rosgen training. At local and regional meetings about specific restoration projects or policies, it has become increasingly common for people to introduce themselves by name, place of work, and level of Rosgen courses completed. By providing a source of educational capital that is nationally recognized, Rosgen's short courses smooth and speed the stream restoration market, making it easier for consultants to establish their legitimacy.

Taken together, the lingua franca provided by Rosgen's classification system, the standards of practice provided by the NCD guidelines, and the educational capital provided by his short courses fill the gap left by academics' unwillingness to codify their knowledge and inability to retool the university to meet the training and certification needs of the field. As a result, consulting firms and resource and regulatory agencies throughout the United States are now heavily staffed with people who associate stream restoration with Rosgen and his NCD approach.

This has serious consequences for restoration practitioners with conventional academic training. Even if a request for proposals does not specify that consultants must use NCD, if that is the only method with which the client agency is familiar, then consultants proposing any other approach are fighting an uphill battle. Consultant Steve Gough described a project that had been in litigation for more than a year because ascending levels of the client's supervisors, all of whom had been to Rosgen's Level I course, objected to the fact that Gough did not use NCD: "The case has been settled twice, but each time someone showed up and said, 'Wait a minute, this guy didn't use the Rosgen System? This can't be right!' It's reached the level of absurdity. Another guy comes in the room and says, 'What? You didn't use the Rosgen system!' And everybody goes, 'Oh shit, did you have to say that? Now we have to open it up again.'"[21]

CONCLUSION

In this chapter I analyzed how Rosgen's classification system, design guidelines, and short course series enabled the day-to-day practice of the American stream restoration field, in the process creating the habitus that has come to define it. The broad base of support that enabled Rosgen to challenge his university-based critics on issues of scientific legitimacy is both cause and consequence of the habitus created by the integrally linked production, circulation, and application of his work. Developing the habitus for the field enabled him, in turn, to redefine the types of scientific capital most valuable in the stream restoration field as described in chapter 4 and thus to reconfigure its objective power structure as described in chapter 2.

But developing the field's habitus is not the only source of Rosgen's success. The ways in which that habitus aligned with shifts in broader political economic relations were also critical. I turn now to the political economy of the stream restoration field.

CHAPTER SIX

The Political Economy of Stream Restoration

I feel [about the Rosgen Wars] a little bit like we feel down
here in the South about the Civil War: deep down in our heart
of hearts we have to admit we lost that one; even though our
cause was noble, the conflict was a terrible waste.
— An agency research scientist

The preceding chapters analyzed the dramatic change in the internal power
structure of the stream restoration field, revealed the accusations participants
in the Rosgen Wars level against each other as simultaneous claims to truth
and capital, and described how Rosgen's production of knowledge claims and
means of circulating them set the habitus for the field, enabling its daily practices and promoting the widespread application of his approach. In this chapter
I analyze how broader political-economic relations have strengthened Rosgen's
position, simultaneously setting the conditions for and reinforcing his rise. I
also examine how the production and circulation of NCD shape its application,
arguing that neoliberal environmental management regimes depend on the
production of particular kinds of knowledge. In the second half of the chapter
I turn the tables and use the Rosgen Wars to reflect on the analytic framework
of Bourdieu's field concept, arguing that there are a few key ways in which it
should be reworked for use by political ecologists and science and technology
studies scholars.

POLITICAL-ECONOMIC INFLUENCES ON THE STREAM RESTORATION FIELD

Political economy focuses on the profound interconnections among policy,
distribution of wealth, and economic development and change. To analyze the
political economy of stream restoration, I assess how state and federal environ-

mental policies create and shape restoration markets, which in turn influence the development of internal agency policy and the actions of agency staff.

Bourdieu incorporates political-economic relations into field analysis through examination of what he describes as the *relative autonomy* of the field. To recap, according to Bourdieu, any field is structured between poles he defines as autonomous and heteronomous (figure 1.5). At the *autonomous* end are those actors whose production is controlled most thoroughly by the pursuit of capital specific to that field; at the *heteronomous* end are those whose production is shaped primarily by outside forces. The relative autonomy of a field can be measured by "the extent to which it manages to impose its own norms and sanctions on the whole set of producers" (Bourdieu 1983, 321). Put differently, a highly autonomous field would be structured in large part by its internal politics (e.g., Renaissance art history), while in a field with relatively little autonomy, the habitus and preeminent forms of capital would be heavily influenced by external demands from state power and economic capital (e.g., computer science).[1]

How autonomous is the stream restoration field? How much influence does the larger political-economic context within which stream restoration is embedded have in the field? How has that influence changed over time?

Policy and Economic Influences

Environmental policy has played a central role in the Rosgen Wars through both formal legislation and the internal policies of resource and regulatory agencies. Many examples of such support have been woven throughout the book, but here I gather some of the most telling together.

As described in chapter 3, federal environmental legislation in the late 1960s and early 1970s played a critical role in the current expansion of the restoration field by shifting the us government from a solely economic view of rivers toward an environmental one. Most notably, the Clean Water Act included regulatory provisions that made stream restoration a condition for obtaining a permit to culvert, channelize, or entirely relocate a stream. This catalyzed the exponential growth of the stream restoration market and of the field more broadly, as staff at federal and state resource agencies, regulators, and anyone wishing to transform an inconveniently located stream abruptly became part of the stream restoration field, drafted in by federal legislation.

In order for this new federal policy imperative to roll out with any smoothness, however, the restoration field needed a structure to shape and unify the social practice of the rapidly expanding field and to enable the exponential

growth of restoration markets necessary to meet these new permit requirements: a system for training the rush of new people joining the field, a shared
language to enable communication among these disparate new participants, a
way of determining their competency and credibility, and guidelines for restoration practice. In Bourdieu's terms, the burgeoning stream restoration field
needed a subjective structure and the habitus to create it.

Academia, the traditional source of habitus in scientific fields, failed to provide the subjective structure for the field; thus when Rosgen stepped forward
with an alternative approach that could enable the field to function, state and
federal agencies supported the production, circulation, and application of his
work in very powerful ways. As described in chapter 2, the Environmental
Protection Agency paid to send thousands of people to Rosgen courses, both
members of its own staff and employees at other federal, state, and local agencies. In North Carolina this shared training created a powerful consensus in
support of NCD, with almost all state funding and regulatory agencies requiring
use of Rosgen's approach.

The US Forest Service has been another central and consistent source of
support for Rosgen, beginning in the late 1980s with the decision to adopt
Rosgen's classification system as the agency standard rather than sue him for
intellectual property infringement for marketing a system he developed while
working there. As described in chapter 2, in the 1990s the Forest Service took
the unprecedented step of purchasing a copy of Rosgen's first textbook for *every
hydrologist in the agency*. Further, the Forest Service has required thousands of
its employees to attend Rosgen short courses over the last twenty-five years.
Taken together, these actions have created an extraordinary level of consensus
around Rosgen's work within the agency. Forest Service requests for proposals for restoration projects, particularly in the Rocky Mountain states, often
require not only an NCD approach but also completion of at least two levels of
NCD training.

The Natural Resources Conservation Service has been yet another bastion
of support for Natural Channel Design. Rosgen training is the norm among
staff who work on stream restoration projects. Natural Resources Conservation
Service design manuals and funding programs, relied upon by local soil and
water conservation districts throughout rural America, typically specify use of
the Rosgen classification system and NCD approach.

Once federal legislation catalyzed the current rapid growth of the stream
restoration field, the internal policies of federal agencies provided a chorus of
support for Rosgen and his NCD approach that has drowned out the voices of
even the most determined critics. Further, by requiring use of NCD and com-

pletion of Rosgen courses, these agencies have deeply influenced the restoration market, forcing many non-NCD consultants to change approaches or leave the field. A number of the consultants I interviewed have either abandoned public sector restoration work or left the field entirely, and restoration firms that use NCD as a central pillar of practice, such as KCI, Stantec, and J. F. New, are booming.

Neoliberalism and the Stream Restoration Field

Since the late 1990s the political-economic framework shaping the production, circulation, and application of stream restoration knowledge claims has been increasingly shaped by neoliberal philosophies. The *interrelated neoliberalization of science and environmental management* powerfully boosted Rosgen's legitimacy and supported the spread of his work, so that by the early to mid-2000s Rosgen's position at the top of the restoration hierarchy was firmly established (figure 3.3). I point here to three key shifts that reflect the rising influence of neoliberal philosophies: the increasing privatization of knowledge claims in the stream restoration field, a shift toward applied research to meet market and agency demands, and the creation of metrics to enable market-based environmental management.

Privatization of knowledge claims

As I described in chapter 1, one of the central characteristics of neoliberal science regimes is an emphasis on privatizing the production of scientific knowledge. In stark contrast to the near monopoly on status and authority university and federal research agency scientists enjoyed during the second half of the twentieth century, the private sector is increasingly seen as a fully legitimate source of scientific knowledge claims, untainted by its explicitly commercial interests. The increased credibility of knowledge claims produced outside the university boosted Rosgen's authority, as his extra-academic status began to appear at worst insignificant and at best as a market-based validation of his knowledge claims: if he could thrive financially outside the university, it must mean his approach really worked.

The actions of federal agencies provide two examples of this increased credibility of privately produced environmental science. In the mid-2000s Environmental Protection Agency staff commissioned Rosgen to develop the protocol for setting sediment total maximum daily loads (TMDLs) for use *nationwide*. This model is referred to as the Watershed Assessment of River

Stability and Sediment Supply (WARSSS). Underlining the agency's assumption of Rosgen's scientific credibility, it did not require him to collaborate with sediment transport researchers at universities or federal research agencies or even to submit WARSSS to peer review. Instead, the EPA allowed Rosgen to keep the assumptions and models underlying WARSSS proprietary (as are Rosgen's classification system and the NCD approach).

The acceptance of proprietary models for public policy is a notable shift in how regulatory science is produced, circulated (or, rather, not circulated), and applied as well as unmistakable evidence of privatization. Further, while it is not yet clear whether the WARSSS protocol will be widely adopted, the fact that Rosgen, not sediment transport researchers from academia or the research agencies, was commissioned to develop the standards demonstrates the increased legitimacy of privately produced science in the stream restoration field.

A second example comes from the Natural Resources Conservation Service, which infuriated Rosgen's critics by inviting him to write an entire chapter of its eagerly awaited federal handbook, *Stream Restoration Design* (Natural Resources Conservation Service 2007), on his proprietary forty-step NCD approach. Rosgen's was the only chapter of the handbook that advocated a single comprehensive approach rather than a range of possible techniques to address a particular, limited problem. As with WARSSS, Rosgen was not required to submit his work for peer review; strikingly, he was the only contributor to the handbook so exempted. The NRCS did ask two prominent Rosgen critics to review the chapter, but they refused when they were told that Rosgen would not be asked to respond to their comments.[2] Again, this demonstrates the increased status accorded to both private sector production of knowledge and the privatization of knowledge claims under neoliberal science regimes.

Shifting toward applied work to meet market demands

Another key shift is visible in the changing research focus of academics and research agency scientists. Analysis of trends in publication and federal funding shows a clear movement toward more applied work, a central tenet of neoliberal science regimes. Further, quantitative and qualitative data suggest that this shift has occurred in direct response to both the rise of Rosgen and the political-economic trends that supported that rise.

As illustrated in figure 6.1, there were relatively low levels of academic publications on stream restoration through the 1990s, followed by a notable increase that began around 2000 and continues into the present day. The number and

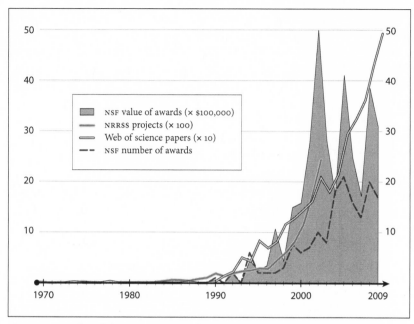

Figure 6.1 Combined data on autonomy of stream restoration field.[3]

total value of National Science Foundation (NSF) grants for research on stream restoration followed the same pattern, remaining relatively low through the late 1990s and then beginning a marked upward trend. Suggestively, these increases in academic research and publication on stream restoration follow shortly after the same exponential growth pattern in number of restoration projects.

Many of my interview subjects confirmed the timing of this trajectory. For example, Peter Wilcock, a sediment transport researcher at Johns Hopkins University, reported that his level of interest in restoration had increased at a couple of key points:

> I initially paid attention, back about . . . [1994/1995], when I first heard people remarking on this Rosgen phenomenon . . . and complaining at scientific meetings about the dumb things that were being done in the name of stream restoration. . . . And then [2002] . . . was the first time that I was actively involved in teaching a restoration short course. I certainly came into that as a sediment transport person. Then my level of activity hit the current maxed-out level [in 2004] when I joined NCED [the National Center for Earth-surface Dynamics]. They decided that stream restoration would be one of three major areas of emphasis and asked me to lead that effort.[4]

Martin Doyle, a geomorphologist at Duke University, described the same timeline from the perspective of someone who had been doing applied work on stream restoration since the mid-1990s, when "the premier geomorphologists in the country were condescending towards river restoration. . . . I distinctly remember telling people I was doing my master's . . . [on stream restoration], and there was definitely a sense of scorning, 'Oh, he's in *applied* fluvial geomorph.'"[5]

Steve Kite, a geomorphologist at West Virginia University and Rosgen Wars moderate, mentioned the effects of both Rosgen and funding availability on the timing of his decision to become involved in stream restoration:

> Can't say as I spent much time thinking about it [stream restoration] until 2001. . . . [S]ome colleagues in the Civil and Environmental Engineering Department had taken his [Rosgen's] courses. They were trying to put together a stream restoration team and found out through networking with a fish biologist that I had worked with that there was a fluvial geomorphologist on campus. That's where my active involvement in restoration started. I had shied away from those sorts of issues for a long time. . . . I realized this was an incredible opportunity to be involved in this [stream restoration]. I said to myself, Not only is this something that's important, it's fundable.[6]

The "fundable" part of this is central: in 1997 the NSF modified its funding criteria to require applicants to justify the importance of the "broader impacts" of their proposed research. As one environmental scientist who reviewed an earlier version of this book pointed out, the addition of the broader-impacts criterion is a result of neoliberalizing science policy in the United States and has certainly been a driver of the shift toward more applied work.

Gary Parker, a sediment transport researcher at the University of Illinois at Urbana-Champaign and, like Kite, a Rosgen Wars moderate, described the relation between the rise of Rosgen and the shift toward applied research among agency and university researchers in both direct and approving terms: "Until Rosgen started actually doing things, most academics had not the slightest intention of getting involved in an applied project and saying how things ought to be done. They spent most of their time telling people what they couldn't do. . . . Rosgen has had the effect of moving the entire field of river geomorphology more in the direction of thinking about how to solve practical problems."[7]

A final example comes from Jack Schmidt, a geomorphologist from Utah State University. Schmidt said that he started the restoration short courses at Utah State because the state Department of Natural Resources came to him and said that they were tired of sending all these people out of state to Rosgen classes; since Utah State was a land-grant school, would it provide an alternative? Schmidt now runs the Utah component of the two-level academic short course series described in chapter 5 in direct response to that government request.[8]

Taken together, these qualitative and quantitative data depict one of the common characteristics of neoliberal science regimes: the shift to applied work to meet market demands. While there are still lots of academics training PhD students and working to fill the many gaps in basic knowledge of the ecology, chemistry, and physics of stream systems, there has been a notable shift in focus for many other university- and agency-based scientists. This latter group is attempting to fend off Rosgen and meet the needs of the stream restoration field through more applied research and the development of educational systems and short course series that mimic the form of Rosgen's while providing alternative content.

Market-based environmental management: creating metrics to define commodities

A third example points to the deep interconnections between neoliberal regimes of science and environmental management as the expansion of market-based environmental policy shapes the production of environmental knowledge claims such markets require to function. A core tenet of neoliberal philosophy, as discussed in the introduction, is that markets are better organizers of social and economic life than states (Peck and Tickell 2002; Harvey 2005; Mirowski 2009). Thus one common characteristic of neoliberal environmental programs and policies has been an emphasis on removing state environmental protection policies and instead attempting to combat environmental degradation by incorporating the natural world into markets (McCarthy and Prudham 2004; Mansfield 2004; Castree 2010). These new markets in ecosystems services, typically established by the state, trade commodities such as carbon credits and constructed wetlands.

In the stream restoration field, the most visible form of neoliberal market-based environmental management is the stream mitigation banking industry. In stream mitigation banking (smb), bankers buy property with damaged streams and restore or enhance those streams to produce mitigation credits on a speculative basis. Developers and public works agencies can then purchase credits to fulfill their permit conditions under the Clean Water Act rather than having to carry out restoration themselves, a time-consuming project with unpredictable outcomes. Although the first stream mitigation bank was established only in 2000, heavy promotion by the EPA has led to the rapid spread of smb throughout the United States.

The key to SMB is establishing ecological equivalence between the stream to be destroyed and the stream to be restored. It is here that *neoliberal environmental management ties directly into neoliberal science regimes*, because assuring equivalence between ecological impact and mitigation is a task of measurement. The SMB industry, like any other market in ecosystem services, depends on environmental scientists to create relatively simple metrics to reliably define mitigation credits, the commodity at the center of stream mitigation banking. These metrics attempt to express the complexities of stream systems in simple schemes that can be used to convert riparian ecosystems into credits that can be sorted, certified, and sold as commodities. Developing agreed-upon, consistent standards of measurement is thus critical to any state's mitigation banking system.

However, as Robertson (2006) has pointed out in relation to wetlands mitigation banking (on which SMB is modeled), developing metrics that are capable of establishing a pared-down equivalency between highly complex systems while remaining ecologically coherent is difficult, perhaps impossible. This creates a serious barrier to the expansion of ecosystem service markets: without codified, simplified metrics, such markets cannot function.

University- and agency-based river scientists share the reluctance and inability of their wetlands-focused colleagues to codify their knowledge into commodity-defining metrics. Yet SMB is in a position different from that of wetlands mitigation banking because the metrics needed to commodify streams were *not only available but already in widespread use* before the first stream mitigation bank opened for business. Despite the objections of public sector scientists and the fact that Rosgen himself argues that it was not designed for such use, his classification system is the central metric used to establish the equivalence of destroyed and restored streams and thus create stream credits for sale in most states' SMB industries.

The Rosgen classification system provides a relatively simple bundled metric for converting the messy reality of streams into easily tradable commodities. Credits are determined based on linear feet of particular Rosgen channel type. For example, if a developer sought a permit to destroy four hundred meters of E4 channel, he or she would be required to purchase credits for four hundred to twelve hundred meters of E4 channel, depending on ratios set by each state. In most states, little attention is paid to the relationship between the scale of the destroyed and restored channels or their particular ecological functions, as they are not included in the Rosgen classification system. Instead, channel form is treated as a proxy for ecological function based on the assumption that if bankers get the form of the channel right, the rest will follow; this is the "*Field of Dreams* hypothesis" typical of NCD referred to in chapter 4.

University- and agency-based scientists have opposed the use of Rosgen's classification system in SMB both because of their general opposition to use of his work and for the more specific reason, discussed in chapter 4, that they do not believe channel form is an adequate proxy for the entire range of ecological characteristics of any given stream. In response, some academics and agency researchers have begun to discuss the possibility of developing new metrics that separate out individual ecosystem services, such as water temperature and mussel habitat, rather than using one combined measurement as a proxy.

Attempting to replace Rosgen's classification system with new metrics that separate ecosystem functions appears problematic to many of his critics, though, because the prevailing paradigm in river science views ecosystem functions as deeply interdependent. How can water quality be separated from endangered species survival? But more specific replacement metrics become more appealing as long-term monitoring data suggest that projects constructed under the current Rosgen-based metrics thus far are failing to restore ecological function.[9] At least with unbundled measures, Rosgen's critics could be sure that *some* ecological functions were being addressed. Further, development of new, more ecologically specific metrics would require research, which might help university- and agency-based scientists reassert their authority in the stream restoration field.

This potential new source of legitimacy, however, would come at the cost of placing academic and agency researchers more firmly in the service of neoliberal environmental management: to develop unbundled metrics for SMB, scientists at universities and research agencies would have to focus their efforts on an agenda determined by the needs of the SMB market. Thus while it might shift the center of gravity of restoration science back toward the public sector, developing replacement metrics would reinforce the trend toward applied research focused on topics of interest to the restoration industry and regulatory agencies.

Clearly, this is a complex set of circumstances to which I cannot do full justice here. But the take-home point is this: *the neoliberal emphasis on market-based environmental management both is dependent on and reinforces the neoliberalization of the production of scientific knowledge claims.* The SMB industry could not function without the codified metrics that Rosgen developed, and these metrics have received crucial support from the same political-economic forces promoting SMB in the first place. Further, the centrality of Rosgen's classification system to the burgeoning SMB market increases its legitimacy and expands its use (Lave, Robertson, and Doyle 2008; Lave, Doyle, and Robertson 2010). Rosgen's success and the neoliberalization of science management in the United States have already started to pull his critics into more applied, market-focused research. To combat his influence in the mitigation banking industry, university- and agency-based researchers would have to produce codified, easily circulatable, and applicable knowledge claims of their own, thus moving into even more market-based realms.

This is just one example of the deep interdependencies between environmental policy and the production of environmental science, but it strongly suggests that understanding the neoliberalization of either environmental science or environmental policy requires analyzing their *interactions*. To rephrase Noel Castree's definition, neoliberalism is simultaneously a social, environmental, and *intellectual* project (2008, 143).

The Relative Autonomy of the Stream Restoration Field

The stream restoration field at the time of this writing is not the same as it was in the early to mid-1990s. It is far bigger and far more heavily influenced by political-economic forces. Further, the stream restoration field has increasingly been characterized by the fight over Rosgen's work, a fight that university- and agency-based researchers are thus far losing. To be clear, it is not the case that Rosgen created a field and now academics and agency researchers want a piece of it. The stream restoration field is more than a century old. The work of university- and agency-based scientists formed its intellectual core during most of that time, and scientists themselves occupied the highest tiers until fairly recently. This makes Rosgen's status even more striking, as he had to displace others to gain it. Political-economic forces have clearly played a role in this shift, providing key support for Rosgen's classification system, design guidelines, and short course series and pulling academic and agency scientists into more applied pursuits. The changes in the relative autonomy and objective power structure of the stream restoration field are clearly interrelated.

REFLECTING ON BOURDIEU THROUGH THE LENS OF THE ROSGEN WARS

Bourdieu's field framework has proved quite useful in explaining the Rosgen Wars and the startling reversal of the typical dynamics of scientific authority within the stream restoration field. Mapping out the objective power structure of the stream restoration field helped explain why Rosgen's critics have engaged him with such passion: within any field, authority is a zero-sum game; no one succeeds without deposing someone else. Instead of being able to comfortably ignore Rosgen, university- and agency-based scientists have been forced to fight in response to loss of stature in the field. The strangely repetitive character of the critics' and supporters' claims and the puzzling absence of attempts to determine whether or not NCD actually works make far more sense when analyzed in Bourdieu's terms as simultaneous substantive critiques and assertions of capital. Because the preeminent forms of capital in a field effectively define its power structure, debates over truth are also attempts to establish authority.

Analysis of the habitus and subjective structure of the stream restoration field began to explain why Rosgen has become so influential. In providing a lingua franca and standards of practice for the field, Rosgen created the systems of perception, training, and certification of capital on which the implementation of restoration policy and markets depend and thus the habitus that shapes the restoration field. Beyond this, Bourdieu frequently observed that *the power of subjective structures is particularly notable when they line up with the objective structure of society as a whole*, so that our categories of perception accord with the power relations they describe. Thus the analysis of the relative autonomy of the field is the final piece needed to explain Rosgen's success: the neoliberalization of science and environmental policy aligned with ways in which Rosgen's knowledge claims are produced, circulated, and applied, reinforcing the shifts in habitus and power relations they created.

There are, however, two key moments where Bourdieu's field concept comes up short: his theorization of how conflicts are settled, particularly the factors that determine whether someone is a significant player, and his conceptualization of the bounded nature of fields.

Settling Conflicts: Who Matters

Bourdieu expends a great deal of effort describing dueling claims to authority and status in different fields, but he never goes into much detail about what allows a particular set of claims and capitals to *win*. There are a few general statements; for example: "In the scientific field as in the field of class relations, no arbitrating authority exists to legitimate legitimacy-giving authorities; claims of legitimacy draw their legitimacy from the relative strength of the groups whose interests they express" (Bourdieu 1975, 24).

But what confers that relative strength in the first place? What are the mechanisms for winning such a fight? And where does change start? The rough outlines of an answer to the last of these questions seems to lie in Bourdieu's argument that subjective structures have the most force when they align with the objective structure of society as a whole, creating categories of perception that harmonize with the power relations they describe. This would suggest that subjective structure is the key entrance point for reshaping a field, and analysis of the Rosgen Wars and their relationship with the neoliberal restructuring of society that began in the late 1970s supports this.

A further critical question, however, is, What makes a person or institution strong enough to establish a different subjective structure and reshape a field? Bourdieu consistently argues that only those participants who hold substantial amounts of capital can be considered to exist in the field in any substantive sense; for example: "As accumulated scientific resources increase, so the incorporated scientific capital needed in order to appropriate them and thereby gain access to scientific problems and tools, and thus to the scientific struggle, becomes greater and greater (the cost of entry). The consequence is that scientific revolution is the business not of the poorest but of the richest (in scientific capital) among the new entrants" (1975, 33).

The Rosgen Wars problematize this view of which participants have the capacity to win a conflict in two quite different ways. First, there is Rosgen himself. Bourdieu argues that the habitus an agent brings into the field profoundly determines the position and trajectory he or she is likely to take within it:

> In a given state of the field, researchers' investments depend both in their amount . . . and their nature . . . on the amount of actual and potential recognition-capital which they possess, and on their actual and potential positions in the field. . . . [Thus] researchers' aspirations . . . rise as their capital of recognition rises. . . . [I]nsofar as the qualification [academic degree], as scholastic capital reconvertible into . . . scientific capital, contains a probable trajectory, it governs the agent's whole relationship with his scientific career (the choice of more or less "ambitious" projects, greater or lesser productivity, etc.) through the intermediary of the "reasonable aspirations" which it authorizes. (1975, 27–28)

According to this description of the powerfully determining relationship between the dispositions that people bring to a field and the positions they assume within it, Rosgen should not exist. In Bourdieu's framing, when Rosgen entered the field he did not hold sufficient amounts of scientific habitus or educational capital to be a contender for greatness or a legitimate combatant in the constant struggle to define the field itself. As demonstrated by Bernhardt et al. (2005), the field of stream restoration began to expand rapidly in the mid-1980s just as Rosgen was starting his consulting and educational work. Given the number of people joining the field at that time, many of whom brought with them prestigious educational qualifications and a great deal of basic scientific capital, it is hard to imagine an interpretation that would view Rosgen — fresh from dismissal by the US Forest Service, with only a BS from Humboldt State University and a determinedly maverick stance — as comparatively rich in scientific capital. Yet despite entering the field with a relatively low stock of capital, Rosgen still managed to grasp the resources needed to mount a powerful challenge to those at the top of the hierarchy when he arrived. Bourdieu's assertion that the dispositions an agent brings into the field determine his trajectory within it is refuted by the current state of the stream restoration field.

Second, the critical role played by both grassroots demand for stream restoration and the broad NCD community suggests that to understand how conflicts are resolved we need to pay attention to those low-level participants in a field who, according to Bourdieu, do not hold sufficient amounts of capital to have any importance within it. As I described in chapter 2, the most basic goals for stream restoration in the United States are deeply contradictory. More than any other type of ecological restoration, human economic needs are a critical component of stream restoration even though they often undermine or obstruct the ecological goals for a project. By setting a Janus-faced foundation for stream restoration (the fundamentally conflicting goals of protecting human economic interests and promoting natural self-determination), the grassroots movement at the base of the stream restoration field helped to set the conditions for Rosgen's success by privileging solutions that offered naturalization and control simultaneously.

Similarly, the power of the relatively powerless — in the form of the mass of practitioners and agency staff who make up the lower tiers of the stream restoration field — was a key factor in Rosgen's success. As they proposed, funded, designed, and reviewed projects, wrote requests for proposals, and selected consultants, these low-level participants made the thousands of minor daily decisions that in aggregate have determined the outcome of the Rosgen Wars thus far. Linked by a shared NCD-based habitus, their individual decisions worked together to effectively set stream restoration policy in the United States and became a force that reoriented the field. Bourdieu's field framework must be expanded to address the role of the uncapitalized masses in determining the outcomes of battles of the capitalized elite.[10]

The Bounded Character of Fields

The second weakness that analysis of the Rosgen Wars exposes lies in the way Bourdieu conceptualizes the fundamental structure of the field. According to Bourdieu, every field is a *bounded* entity related to the field of power (as evi-

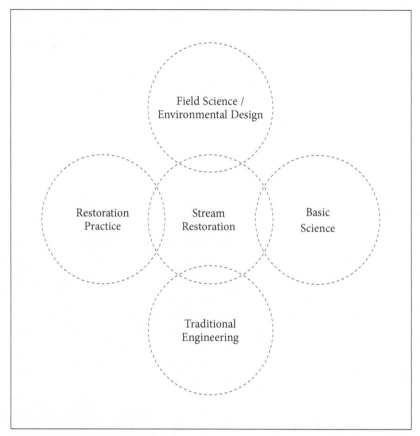

Figure 6.2 Relations among fields.

denced in the axis from autonomous to heterogeneous production) but not to other fields. Thus in Bourdieu's terms, the obvious read on the Rosgen Wars would be a struggle between autonomy (university- and agency-based scientists) and heterogeneity (Rosgen and his attention to regulatory and market demands). And yet, as shown in figure 3.3, it is inaccurate to characterize Rosgen as the heteronomous pole of the field and the Rosgen Wars as simply a fight over whether stream restoration will be defined by its own internal goals or by the goals of markets and the state. Although I have argued that the demands of government agencies and the restoration market were fundamental to Rosgen's success, his work is not driven only by the goal of meeting those demands. According to Rosgen and his supporters, the types of scientific capital that define the stream restoration field and grant their holders legitimacy and expert status are fundamentally about field science, success in hands-on work, and correspondence with nature. While this list displays a wide range of influences from other fields, they are not mere measures of market-based success or satisfaction of state goals.

Instead, the confusion over where Rosgen and the NCD community stand on the autonomy/heteronomy axis demonstrates a larger issue: that Bourdieu defines production determined by the core values of the field as *autonomous*, bounded off from other fields. In contrast to this contained vision, a major part of what is at stake in the Rosgen Wars is the question of *which* outside fields should serve as the polestars orienting the field's axis (figure 6.2). For the university- and agency-based scientists who until the mid-1990s dominated the US stream restoration field, its key relation is with the more rarefied field of basic science; the types of capital they privilege are all derived from orthodox scientific practice. By contrast, Rosgen's push to reorient the field seems to be based on the belief that stream restoration should have stronger ties to the environmental and applied science fields, as is evident from the types of capital he and his supporters prioritize. The Rosgen Wars thus demonstrate that the core values of a field can be, and perhaps always are, determined *in relation* to other fields rather than in the isolation that Bourdieu's term *autonomy* implies.

CHAPTER SEVEN

Conclusions

The unusual state of the American stream restoration field raises some critical questions. First, why was Rosgen able to establish himself as the most scientifically legitimate expert in the stream restoration field — the primary trainer of practitioners and the developer of the most broadly accepted knowledge claims about how streams, and thus restoration projects, work — in the face of determined opposition from the scientific establishment? Second, why does that opposition exist, particularly given the lack of definitive evidence that the NCD approach is fundamentally flawed, and why has it persisted despite a consistent lack of results?

As I have described in the preceding chapters, the answer to the first question is primarily political-economic, as environmental regulation and the needs of agency staff and restoration markets played a key role in Rosgen's rise. Landmark environmental legislation was a powerful catalyst to the enormous expansion of the restoration field, which began in the 1980s. In turn, this growth created great demand for restoration training, a lingua franca to enable communication among the disciplines involved in restoration science and practice, and standards of practice to guide project managers' selection of approaches and consultants, as described in chapter 5. The subjective structure that developed around Rosgen's work powerfully promoted his scientific authority and knowledge claims, as federal agencies sent thousands of people to his courses, specified his methods in RFPs and manuals, and lent credibility to the types of capital he possessed.

The codified form of Rosgen's knowledge claims and their circulation through short courses played, and continues to play, a crucial enabling role for the restoration market. As described in chapter 5, Rosgen became the key provider of the educational capital that allowed consultants to assert their legitimacy, which only became more important as the field expanded and the number of firms increased. Further, Rosgen's work is central to the fastest-growing segment of the restoration market: stream mitigation banking. As described in chapter 6, this market-based approach to stream restoration practice is at present deeply dependent on Rosgen's classification system, which serves as the key metric for producing and certifying credits for sale. Restoration consulting firms, developers working to meet permit conditions, and mitigation bankers are all deeply invested in Rosgen's legitimacy and success: without him, market conditions become much less predictable and, in the case of mitigation banking, potentially unfeasible.

A last political-economic aspect of Rosgen's rise comes from the congruence between the neoliberalization of environmental science and policy and the habitus he produced. As Bourdieu pointed out repeatedly in his work on fields, subjective structures are at their most powerful when they align with the objective structure of society more broadly. This suggests that it is no coincidence that the Rosgen Wars coincided with a major shift in the structure of American political economy with the rise of neoliberalism. A major source of Rosgen's success is the resonance between his work and the neoliberal emphasis on the commercialization and privatization of knowledge.

As described in chapter 1, the rise of neoliberal science management regimes has created a decisive and substantive shift in the organization and practice of science in the United States. The key features of the neoliberalization of American academia thus far include a dramatic increase in dependence on private funding for universities and research, the aggressive commercialization of knowledge through a striking expansion of intellectual property protection, a shift toward more applied work produced to enable the new markets created by neoliberal policies, and an increasing reliance on market take-up to adjudicate substantive intellectual disputes.

As described in chapter 6, many of these trends are clearly visible in the stream restoration field. River scientists are shifting to more applied work in response to the demands of agencies with increasingly neoliberal agendas, markets created by government regulation (such as stream mitigation banking), and the rise of Rosgen. Rosgen (a private producer of commercialized science) and his NCD approach (a privately produced, proprietarily held set of knowledge claims prepared to serve state and market needs) embody the neoliberal trends described above. Further, Rosgen's commercial success is widely viewed as *validating* the strength of his knowledge claims, while university- and agency-based scientists' claims are viewed as less legitimate because of their lack of marketable utility for participants in the stream restoration field. Rosgen's success in shifting the internal power relations of the stream restoration field stems from the ways the subjective structure he provided for the stream restoration field harmonizes with the current structure of US society in all its neoliberal glory.

The answer to the second question — why the opposition to NCD has been so ferocious and persistent — springs from the analysis of the objective structure of the field and the forms of capital that define it in chapters 3 and 4. First, as Bourdieu points out, fields are hierarchies, not pluralities: room at the top is limited. Further, the internal power relations of any field are deeply interdependent, causing a particular position in the field to change "whenever there is change in the universe of options that are simultaneously offered for producers and consumers to choose from" (Bourdieu 1983, 312). Thus a crucial reason why academic and agency-based scientists bothered to engage Rosgen was that he shifted their positions simply by entering the field, calling their authority into question without doing, or even intending to do, anything to them. As the analysis of objective structure mapped in figures 3.2 and 3.3 illustrates, intentionally or not, Rosgen's success displaced his critics from the apex of the field to a far less prestigious location. Supporting this analysis, Martin Doyle, a geomorphologist at Duke University, pointed out that top scientists in the restoration field only began to engage in the Rosgen Wars when, in the early 2000s, they "started hearing from their students who are now consulting that they weren't being considered qualified to do river work. . . . I think that's what got [them] . . . involved: being told that they're not qualified to do things."[1]

Further, analysis in chapter 4 of the debate over Rosgen's work revealed the fight to be not simply an intellectual battle over opposing truth claims but also the primary avenue through which Rosgen's critics continue to press their claims to authority and to argue for the importance of the types of scientific capital they hold. The struggle for status within the field and the struggle to valorize the types of capital held by particular types of participants are one and the same.

Thus with the modifications described in the last section of chapter 6, field analysis revealed that Rosgen's success and his opposition's fury are two faces of the same coin, forged together in profoundly relational ways. Rosgen's ability to meet the needs of restoration markets and agencies reshaped the field's subjective structure in ways that accorded well with the larger neoliberal structure of society as a whole, leading in turn to a dramatic reorientation of the power structure of the stream restoration field and thus to a revaluation of the types of capital that define it.

THE FUTURE OF STREAM RESTORATION

Where does the stream restoration field go from here? Throughout my research I paid particular attention to discussions of the likely trajectory of the Natural

Channel Design approach. Interestingly, many of Rosgen's opponents and his supporters feel that NCD is destined to lose its current prominence.

Rosgen's supporters and some moderates point to two factors that might cause NCD's popularity to fade: Rosgen's retirement and the rise of new methods. Rosgen is nearly seventy years old, and he works at a pace most people would find unsustainable in their twenties. It is not clear how long he can maintain it, and yet doing so is considered critical by many of his supporters because they see his knowledge and charisma as central to the appeal of his work. Many speculated that attendance at short courses would drop dramatically if Rosgen no longer taught them, with a resulting reduction in agencies and consultants employing his methods. At that point, speculation goes, other promising restoration methods would gain prominence in their turn. As Gary Parker, a sediment transport researcher at the University of Illinois and Rosgen Wars moderate, put it, "You know what's gonna happen: . . . Dave's gonna retire. . . . He's getting older, and he's teaching at an exhausting pace. I can't even imagine how he does it. When he tapers off, he has been *the* person doing this. . . . I know he has people working with him at Wildland Hydrology, but I very much doubt that they have the charisma that he does. So it might taper off then, and we might see other things rising."[2] This almost Weberian vision of charismatic authority misreads the deeper roots of Rosgen's success. Clearly, Rosgen's charisma is not trivial, but focusing on the man hides the far more important function his approach serves in enabling the market, resource management, and regulatory practices of stream restoration.

Rosgen's critics have a different vision of how NCD's prominence may wane. They point to what they consistently describe as the "life cycle" of adoption, often based on what happened in Maryland: first, agencies enthusiastically embrace the NCD approach based on claims of universal applicability, doability, and stability and fund a plethora of NCD projects; at some point thereafter, a five-to-ten-year storm hits, and there is a rash of dramatic project failures; finally, agencies come to their senses and start looking for other approaches. As critic Martin Doyle described it, "It seems like there's a life cycle: love Rosgen, get overenamored with him, start to see some failures and shortcomings of the approach, and then start to do other things. . . . Tennessee has just gotten into river restoration in the last five years, and they're all about Rosgen. So I figure they've got another three to five years before they start to come down off the high."[3]

Both of these predictions, supporters' and critics', ignore the central role that Rosgen's work plays in the stream restoration field. It is difficult to imagine the stream restoration field's exponential growth since the 1980s without the lingua franca, standards of practice, training, and key metrics that Rosgen's work provides. Thus I would suggest a third possible trajectory: adaptation and expansion. My data from North Carolina support this.

As I described in chapter 3, North Carolina is a bastion of support for the NCD approach. But upon closer examination, the picture is more complicated. The local, state, and federal agency staff members I interviewed, almost all of whom used NCD, tended to have well-thought-out critiques of it (table 7.1).[4] The most common were that NCD is often applied thoughtlessly and that it does not apply well to the particular conditions either in North Carolina as a whole or in urban conditions in particular. Other criticisms included the narrow focus on the project reach and the lack of attention to biology. These criticisms should sound familiar: they are common objections raised by NCD critics, as discussed in chapter 4. Only two of the twenty North Carolinians I interviewed said Rosgen's approach had no weaknesses, which contrasts sharply with the image of Rosgen supporters as mindless members of the Cult of Dave.

Further, interview subjects' balanced view of the strengths and weaknesses of the NCD approach has produced changes in their practice. The restoration community in North Carolina may use NCD almost to a person, but many of them are adapting it to address local conditions and broader concerns. For example, Will Harman, one of the founding principals of Buck Engineering, a top NCD consulting firm, said that he has modified the reference reach aspect of Rosgen's approach to fit local conditions because he came to realize that

> all of our reference reaches . . . were in mature, bottomland hardwood forest, one-hundred-year-old forest, fifty-year-old at least, and that pattern was really dictated by that vegetation. . . . They are not "free to form channels" like they have out in the arid West, where vegetation doesn't play a key role because it's so slow in establishing that the river sort of establishes its pattern first. . . . That's not really the case here. . . . [In contrast,] we are working in a denuded floodplain, and when we would try to put in the radius of curvature that worked great in that reference setting where there's a fifty-year-old oak tree holding the bend in place, now we've got nothing but some root wads or a cross-vane or something [to hold things in place], and life taught us better. So . . . we've really modified that approach.[5]

Harman is not alone in modifying the NCD approach. A majority of those employing NCD in North Carolina said that they were supplementing it with additional restoration approaches. Figure 7.1 shows that while 35 percent of respondents were using NCD as their sole restoration method, 40 percent were adding other approaches to a primary focus on NCD, and 15 percent were using

Table 7.1. Weaknesses of Rosgen's approach

New and untested	10%
No consideration of biology	10%
Limits focus to project reach	15%
Expensive	25%
Often poorly implemented	25%
Not applicable here without modification	30%
Applied thoughtlessly	35%
No answer	10%

Note: Percentages do not sum to 1 because respondents frequently mentioned more than one concern.

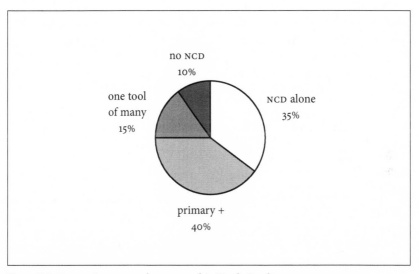

Figure 7.1 Restoration approaches reported in North Carolina.

NCD as simply one of many tools in their toolkit. Additional restoration techniques employed included careful attention to aquatic habitat, sophisticated hydraulic modeling, broad drainage basin–scale analysis of land-use factors causing channel change, adaptation to regional climate and geology, and even a move toward more deformable treatments. In fact, many of the changes that Rosgen's critics say must be made to correct his work seem to already be in process in North Carolina. Dick Everhart, one of the primary supporters of NCD in North Carolina, said he tells students in his workshops "to keep your eyes open and continue to learn. If it works, try to refine it; if it fails, try to figure out why. . . . If you don't keep learning, you're not doing your job!"[6]

Thus in contrast to both Rosgen's supporters and his opponents, I think that twenty years from now most practitioners in the United States will describe themselves as using Natural Channel Design, but Rosgen's contribution to that approach will be increasingly peripheral.

For the moment, however, evidence from the regulatory arena suggests that Rosgen's prominence is not likely to peak any time soon. As mentioned in chapter 6, the EPA is promoting Rosgen's Watershed Assessment of River Stability and Sediment Supply approach as its recommended method for setting total maximum daily loads (TMDLs) for sediment nationwide. This has the potential to vastly expand the reach of Rosgen's work from the large but still limited pool of wadeable streams perceived to be in need of restoration to all flowing bodies of water in the United States. Further, the stream mitigation banking industry, also described in chapter 6, is largely dependent on Rosgen's classification system to provide the metrics critical to enable recent neoliberal incursions into stream restoration. The stream mitigation banking industry is growing rapidly; thus it, too, seems likely to ensure Rosgen's centrality for some time to come.

BRIDGING POLITICAL ECOLOGY AND STS

A primary theoretical goal for this book was to bridge political ecology and science and technology studies. The reason there have been so many calls to build such a bridge is not (or at least not only) the pursuit of academic novelty: traditional models of the production, circulation, and application of science are not adequate (figure 1.1). There are at least two reasons for moving to a more complex relational model (figure 1.4).

The Rosgen Wars demonstrate that, contrary to the commonsense view, the production, circulation, and application of science are deeply interconnected. As described in the preceding chapters, Rosgen produces his knowledge claims with circulation and application in mind, crafting his classification system and standards of practice into codified, efficiently teachable, and easily applicable forms. Similarly, Rosgen circulates his knowledge claims — via short courses and a packaged set of techniques — in ways designed to meet the demand of consultants and agency employees for easily implementable restoration tools, accessible restoration education, and educational capital. These profound interrelations among what are typically thought of as separate stages of the knowledge transmission process seem to be more common than not. For example, James Evans (2010) demonstrates that how scientific knowledge claims are produced — whether in private or public labs — has a statistically significant impact on when and how they are circulated and used.

Further, the same types of political-economic forces that political ecologists see at work in the circulation and application of environmental science (figure 1.2) also affect its production. The Rosgen Wars demonstrate this, as the production, dissemination, and use of Rosgen's knowledge claims, not to mention his overall success, are shaped by political-economic forces. There are many other striking examples of the influence of political-economic relations on the production of science. Jill Fisher (2009) has recently demonstrated that clinical trials in the United States are disproportionately filled with low-income patients who could not otherwise afford health care of any kind; the same players that shut low-income Americans out of access to health care — the insurance and pharmaceutical industries — generate profit by using their bodies to produce scientific claims and medical products. Similarly, Chris Duvall (2011) demonstrates how the production of soil science in Africa has been intimately tied to colonial and neocolonial goals of controlling natural resources and recalcitrant populations. Clearly, unequal power relations and political-economic forces can impact all three stages of knowledge transmission.

Thus an analytical framework that reveals the profound interconnections among the production, circulation, and application of scientific knowledge and the role that political-economic forces play in all three is important *intellectually* because it reveals the work that science does in the world. Such an analytical framework can also be important *politically* in exposing relations of power and domination in which science plays a role.

CRITICAL PHYSICAL GEOGRAPHY

While this book draws primarily on social science methods and analysis, my research in fluvial geomorphology also deeply informs it. This is most explicit in chapter 4, where I assess the claims for and against Natural Channel Design. Without my knowledge of geomorphology and restoration science and practice, it would have been impossible for me to uncover the profound lack of evidence to support many of the claims and counterclaims in the Rosgen Wars. And yet this lack of evidence is the foundation of my argument. There would be little interest in the Rosgen Wars outside the stream restoration field if they were only a clearly resolvable fight over truth.

To get past the framework of claim versus counterclaim, my analysis *required* both natural and social science. And it is here that my third critique of Bourdieu's field concept comes into focus: using it in future analysis of the political economy of the production and use of science will require more attention to the substantive content of science. While Bourdieu alienated many in the STS community by critiquing their strong constructivist program, he himself was still far more interested in the structure and organization of the scientific field than in the knowledge claims made within it. By contrast, I argued in this book that those substantive claims can be critical to both the structure and the autonomy of a scientific field.

To pick just one example outside of stream restoration, the current broad consensus in ecology around the ecosystem services paradigm has powerful economic and environmental consequences (Bellamy Foster 2002; Palmer and Filoso 2009; Robertson 2006; Vira and Adams 2009). To understand where that consensus came from, the analyst must assess how it was shaped by both the internal power structures of the ecological field and the external political-economic influences that shape its autonomy. To do so requires the *ecological* knowledge to understand and assess the truth claims at the heart of the eco-system services paradigm and a deep *political-economic* engagement to understand why they matter (see Robertson et al. [in review] for an example of this combined approach). Thus I hope that demonstrating the utility of combining natural and critical social science research in this book will encourage other critical geographers and environmental scientists to move toward more trans-disciplinary research.

THE POLITICAL ECONOMY OF ENVIRONMENTAL SCIENCE

The Rosgen Wars have serious implications not just for the ways in which we *study* science but also for the *practice* of environmental science. Rosgen's work demonstrates the possibility that the center of scientific legitimacy may switch to the private sector. He has transcended the consultant's traditional role as applier of knowledge developed within academia, creating a classification system for ordering new data, developing and promulgating a set of knowledge claims about how best to understand riparian ecosystems, and building an educational system for circulating those claims that has gradually superseded the American university system. He has ascended to the peak of the restoration field (more accurately, he arrived somewhere and successfully declared it the peak) with little formal academic training, without conforming to many of the established norms of scientific practice, and without support from the official gatekeepers of scientific authority. Further, to combat his influence, public sector river science has shifted toward applied work. Thus not only has the scientific center of gravity of the stream restoration field shifted, but academic practice has changed as well.

Is this a fluke, or are the Rosgen Wars a portent of larger trends in the environmental sciences? There is no sure answer to this question, but my sense is that the Rosgen Wars do indeed presage a larger shift in the political economy of environmental science as a result of the intersection of the United States' increasingly neoliberal regime of science management and the particular character of environmental science itself.

As described in the introduction, neoliberal science regimes are quite distinct from the previous Cold War science management regime, with impacts including steep reductions in public funding, an intense focus on the commercialization of knowledge, and a shift toward more applied research topics. Environmental sciences may be particularly open to neoliberalization because they both address issues with intense economic significance and are, relatively speaking, less able to defend their boundaries from private incursions.

While the particular politics of the stream restoration field are unusual, it has some important commonalities with other newly prominent environmental sciences, such as the study of climate change and the impacts of environmental mutagens. First, like stream restoration, these fields are driven by the normative environmental commitments and perceptions of crisis of the public and of scientists themselves rather than by scientific breakthroughs. They thus are characterized by their relatively undeveloped content, often drawn from pieces of existing fields and not yet fully integrated. Second, like stream restoration, these fields both study highly complicated systems and are based on new scientific paradigms that emphasize complexity. This gives their findings a high level of uncertainty that is not commensurate with the expected role of science as arbiter of truth in the policy process; as I noted in chapter 4, it has so far been impossible to prove whether or not Natural Channel Design actually works in part because of the complexity of the systems involved. Third, like stream restoration, the new environmental sciences deal with issues in which the general population has powerful interests. People want to be able to control the consequences of potential crises from flooding or climate change; thus they may intervene in scientific debates to support solutions they believe address their needs. In many cases the new environmental sciences deal with issues that are similarly central to developing or established markets, which adds to the demand for certainty. I am thinking here of the stream mitigation banking industry (Lave, Robertson, and Doyle 2008; and Lave, Doyle, and Robertson

2010) and the growing weather derivatives (Randalls 2010) and carbon markets (Cooper 2010).

Thus the relative lack of substantive development compared to older, more established fields, the complexity of the systems studied, and the intensity of the human interests involved render the environmental sciences far less able to police their boundaries and fend off knowledge claims from outside the traditional scientific realm. At present, these outside claims seem to be gaining strength through the neoliberal emphasis on private and commercialized knowledge, which makes outsiders offering applied science solutions look increasingly credible.

This strongly suggests that the implications of the Rosgen Wars are not limited to the stream restoration field but instead presage a fundamental shift in the political economy of environmental science. What remains to be seen are the consequences of this shift for the content of science and the justice of the ends it serves. As the Rosgen Wars illustrate, it is not yet clear whether science developed in opposition to the academy will turn out to be beneficial or harmful (or both). Perhaps privatization and commercialization will open up the formerly heavily bounded scientific field to outsiders with different ideas and political agendas, in which case the neoliberal forces integral to Rosgen's rise could turn out to have a notable silver lining.

APPENDIX

Interview and Survey Metadata

SEMISTRUCTURED INTERVIEW SUBJECTS

I conducted semistructured interviews with the following agency staff, consultants, professors, and nonprofit staff. This list does not include subjects interviewed off the record.

Brian Bledsoe, Colorado State University

Margaret Bowman, American Rivers

Karin Boyd, Applied Geomorphology, Inc.

Syd Brown, California Department of Parks and Recreation

John Buffington, us Forest Service

Janine Castro, us Fish and Wildlife Service

Jock Conyngham, us Army Corps of Engineers, Engineer Research and
  Development Center

Brian Dietterick, California Polytechnic Institute, San Luis Obispo

Peter Downs, Stillwater Sciences

Martin Doyle, Duke University

Craig Fishenich, us Army Corps of Engineers, Engineer Research and
  Development Center

Ted Geier, us Forest Service

Scott Gillilan, Gillilan Associates, Inc.

Steve Gough, Little River Consulting

Brian Graber, Massachusetts Waterways

Karen Gran, National Center for Earth-surface Dynamics

Angela Greene, Natural Resources Conservation Service/Canaan
  Valley Institute

Jeffrey Haltiner, Philip Williams & Associates

William Harman, Stream Mechanics

Cheryl Harrelson, Steady Stream Hydrology

Richard Hey, University of Birmingham

Rollin Hotchkiss, Brigham Young University

Greg Jennings, North Carolina State University

Timothy Keane, Kansas State University

Steven Kite, West Virginia University

Greg Koonce, Inter-Fluve, Inc.

Eric Larsen, University of California at Davis

Daniel Levish, Bureau of Reclamation

James MacBroom, Milone & MacBroom

Scott McBain, McBain & Trush

Dale Miller, Mainstream Restoration, Inc.

David Montgomery, University of Washington

Gary Parker, University of Illinois

John Potyondy, US Forest Service

Rhonda Reed, CALFED Bay–Delta Program/National Oceanic and
  Atmospheric Administration

Ann Riley, San Francisco Bay Regional Water Quality Control Board

David Rosgen, Wildland Hydrology

Conor Shea, US Fish and Wildlife Service

Doug Shields, USDA, Agricultural Research Service, National
  Sedimentation Laboratory

Andrew Simon, USDA, Agricultural Research Service, National
  Sedimentation Laboratory

Peter Skidmore, Nature Conservancy/Skidmore Restoration
  Consulting LLC

Louise Slate, Stewart Engineering

Sean Smith, Maryland Department of Natural Resources

Robbin Sotir, Robbin B. Sotir and Associates

Tracy Sylte, US Forest Service

Vaughan Voller, University of Minnesota

Kris Vyverberg, California Department of Fish and Game

Peter Whiting, Case Western Reserve University

Peter Wilcock, Johns Hopkins University

Jim Wilcox, Plumas County Community Development Commission

Laura Wildman, American Rivers

Philip Williams, Philip Williams & Associates

Ellen Wohl, Colorado State University

Because these interviews were semistructured, the questions I asked varied from person to person. However, there were some questions I asked everyone I interviewed and other questions that I asked everyone in a particular group (pro-Rosgen consultants, anti-Rosgen agency staff, etc.).

1. List of common questions asked of all subjects, time permitting:

   - Please give me a brief overview of your education and any previous restoration-related jobs.

   - When and how did you get interested in restoration?

   - When and in what context did you first hear of Dave Rosgen or the Rosgen Method/Natural Channel Design?

   - What has your experience with Rosgen and his work been since then?

   - What do you see as the strengths and weaknesses of the classification system and design approach?

   - What do you believe is at stake in the debate over Rosgen's work?

   - What trajectory do you think the Rosgen Method/Natural Channel Design is on: rising, holding steady, declining in influence?

   - What do you see as the best way to educate restoration practitioners?

   - What do you believe is the current state of restoration science in terms of the relative certainty of practice?

   - Whom should I talk to next?

2. Question for all staff at consulting firms, public agencies, and nonprofits:

   • What is your role at _____ and how does it relate to restoration?

3. Questions for all academics:

   • How have you learned about the content of Rosgen's work?

   • In your classes or short courses do you say anything about Rosgen's work?

   • Have any of your students ever been considered unqualified for a job because they had not been through Rosgen's training?

4. Questions for all consultants:

   • Can you apply the Rosgen classification system?

   • Could you walk me through your design approach?

5. Question for all anti-Rosgen consultants:

   • Have you ever lost a job because of your refusal to use Rosgen's approach?

STRUCTURED INTERVIEWS

I conducted structured interviews about restoration practice in North Carolina with the following people:

Tony Able, Environmental Protection Agency Region 4

Charles Anderson, NRCS/Pilot View Resource Conservation and Development District

Jeff Bruton, North Carolina Department of Water Resources, Water Resources Development Grant Program

Marella Buncick, US Fish and Wildlife Service, Asheville Field Office

John Cox, Durham Stormwater Engineering

Trish D'arconte, Chapel Hill Stormwater Utility

Brady Dodd, us Forest Service

Dick Everhart, NRCS/Surry County Soil and Water Conservation District

Tim Garrett, Southwestern Resource Conservation and Development District

Tom Gerow, North Carolina Division of Forest Resources

Anita Goetz, us Fish and Wildlife Service, Asheville Field Office

Keith Huff, Winston-Salem Stormwater Division

Gary Jordan, us Fish and Wildlife Service, Raleigh Field Office

Jennifer Krupowicz, Charlotte Mecklenberg Stormwater Utility

Eric Kulz, North Carolina Division of Water Quality

Andrea Leslie, Ecosystem Enhancement Program, Western Branch

Callie Moore, Hiwassee River Watershed Coalition

Jeff Parker, Transylvania County Soil and Water Conservation District

David Phlegar, Greensboro Stormwater Management

Alan Walker, Natural Resources Conservation Service

I asked all of these subjects the following set of questions:

1. In what ways is your agency/office involved in stream restoration or channel stabilization work: funding, managing, designing, etc.?

2. Approximately when did your agency first become involved in stream restoration/channel stabilization projects?

3. Why did your agency become involved in stream restoration/ channel stabilization projects?

4. Approximately how many projects are you involved in per year?

5. Have you heard of the Rosgen Method of Natural Channel Design, and if so, in what context?

6. Do you utilize Natural Channel Design in your work? (If *yes*, skip to question 8.)

7a. Did your agency use Natural Channel Design in the past? If so, when, and why did you abandon it?

7b. What approach do you use instead?

8. Why did you select that approach?

9. What are its strengths and weaknesses for your purposes in your day-to-day work?

10. Have you or other staff in your agency attended Rosgen training courses? If so, who, and to what level?

11. At the local scale, which of the following agencies or groups in your area are involved in restoration work? (Please check all that apply. Contact suggestions would be greatly appreciated!)

❏ City public works or planning departments. Suggested contacts: _____

❏ County public works or planning departments. Suggested contacts: _____

❏ Soil and Water Conservation Districts. Suggested contacts: _____

❏ Nonprofit or watershed groups. Suggested contacts: _____

❏ Other.

MAIL SURVEYS OF SHORT COURSE PARTICIPANTS

I sent the following survey questions to all students in the Rosgen Level I course I attended in Santa Cruz, California, in January 2005 and to all the students in the initial academic short course I attended in Bishop, California, in October 2004.

1. Name:

2. When and in what context did you first hear of fluvial geomorphology?

3. Why did you choose this short course?

4. What were your goals for the course?

5. Did the course meet those goals? How?

6. Based on the information presented in the course, how predictable or unpredictable do you think restoration work is? (Please circle the number on the scale below that best applies.)

Unpredictable	Moderately unpredictable	Moderately predictable	Predictable
1 2 3	4 5	6 7 8	9 10

7. Have you used any of the knowledge or skills gained in this course? If yes, please describe.

8. Education: please list any degrees you have completed and the dates when they were earned.

9. Have you taken any restoration-related short courses before or since this course? If yes, please list the courses and their approximate dates.

10. Do you plan to take any additional restoration-related courses? If so, please list the courses you are considering.

11. What is your current role in restoration projects?
    ❏ Designer   ❏ Funder   ❏ Project Manager
    ❏ Other (please explain)

12. Do you work for a:
    ❏ Consulting firm   ❏ Government agency   ❏ Nonprofit
    ❏ Other (please explain)

NOTES

1. Gary Parker, a sediment transport researcher and Rosgen Wars moderate, invited Rosgen over the objections of some participants. As Parker described it, "There was a strong vote to make sure that Rosgen was not invited, but I made damn sure that he was. . . . Academics tend to be somewhat dismissive of Rosgen's approach. Rosgen, however, can accurately be described as one of the founders and certainly the major popularizer of the field of river restoration. To my mind, then, it would be unthinkable not to invite him . . . to a major US workshop on the subject."

CHAPTER ONE. *Introduction*

1. For journal articles critical of Rosgen's work, see Doyle and Harbor (2000); Gillilan (1996); Juracek and Fitzpatrick (2003); Kondolf (1995, 1998); Kondolf, Smeltzer, and Railsback (2001); Miller and Ritter (1996); Roper et al. (2008); Sear (1994); Shields, Brookes, and Haltiner (1999); Simon et al. (2007); and Smith and Prestegaard (2005). For conference presentations, see Ashmore (1999); Doyle, Miller, and Harbor (1999); Kondolf (2007); Shields and Copeland (2006); Simon (2006); Simon et al. (2005); and Simon and Langendoen (2006). For national guidelines unsupportive or actively critical, see Federal Interagency Stream Restoration Working Group (1998); Shields et al. (2003, 2009); and Slate et al. (2007). For white papers on this topic, see Miller, Skidmore, and White (2001).

2. For more on the concept of regimes of science organization, funding, and thought styles, see Mirowski (2011); and Pestre (2003). There are a number of other useful sources on the impact of neoliberalism on science in the United States and abroad. See, for example, Canaan and Shumar (2008); Lave, Mirowski, and Randalls (2010); Mirowski and Plehwe (2009); Nedeva and Boden (2006); Newfield (2008); Nowotny et al. (2005); Pestre (2005); and Slaughter and Rhoades (2002).

3. Before the global financial crisis of 2008, state contributions to budgets of flagship public research universities had shrunk to around 20 percent, but with the current economic contraction, that number has decreased further (Mirowski 2011).

4. This corresponds with Nowotny et al.'s category of Mode 2 knowledge, suggesting that the trends Mirowski finds in the United States are present in the European Union as well.

5. There is more than one way to construct a political-economic span between STS and political ecology. A handful of critical nature/society scholars have built theoretical and empirical connections that do some of the same work in other contexts (Bavington 2010; Randalls 2010; Robertson 2006; Sayre 2008; and Walker and Cooper 2011), and

there are some STS scholars who wield political-economic analyses to great effect (such as Fisher 2009; Mirowski 2011; Mirowski and Plehwe 2009; Pestre 2003, 2005; and Sunder-Rajan 2006). Bourdieu's method is not the only way create a political-economic bridge between STS and political ecology, but his work can be a very effective base from which to build.

6. Like Marx, Bourdieu defines his central analytical concepts relationally. Thus it is impossible to sort out what Bourdieu is trying to accomplish with the idea of the *field* without also addressing the ways in which *habitus* and *capital*, the other two members of his conceptual triumvirate, shape it. For example, fields are defined by the types of capital that are valued within them, while conversely, there is no capital without a field in which to deploy it. Thus the discussion that follows, while holding field at its center, shuttles among all three concepts.

CHAPTER TWO. *Stream Restoration and Natural Channel Design*

1. http://water.epa.gov/action/adopt/index.cfm, accessed July 20, 2010.

2. Some stream scientists are more worried about invasives than others. After all, the biogeography of the planet changed drastically with European colonization, as Alfred Crosby explains in vivid terms in *Ecological Imperialism* (1986), and climate change is already shifting it again. What, then, counts as native?

3. Author interviews with Greg Koonce, principal, Inter-Fluve, Inc., September 14, 2007; James MacBroom, principal, Milone & MacBroom, September 4, 2007; Dale Miller, former principal, Inter-Fluve, Inc., August 31, 2007; Robbin Sotir, principal, Robbin Sotir & Associates, October 1, 2007; and Philip Williams, principal, Philip Williams & Associates, September 11, 2007.

4. I asked about federal agency stances toward NCD in all the interviews I conducted, and the answers were remarkably consistent both among themselves and with the easiest source of verification: the agency homes of authors of pro- and anti-NCD conference presentations and papers.

5. Author interview with John Potyondy, US Forest Service, April 29, 2004.

6. In the United States, contracts to carry out stream restoration work are typically awarded via a competitive bidding process. The project manager, typically employed at a resource agency or NGO, issues a request for proposals, describing the proposed project. Consulting firms then prepare proposals on the basis of which the project manager selects one firm to conduct the work.

7. While Rosgen spends a good deal of time on valley types in his Level I and II courses, first textbook, and field guide, none of the practitioners who use his approach mentioned valley types in my interviews with them.

8. As a final, more detailed step, the classification can include a subletter to describe where in the allowable range of slope for a category a particular channel lies. This produces classifications such as B6a, or C2c-. These subletter classifications are not used frequently. In more than sixty interviews, they were mentioned only twice.

9. Author interview with Dr. Timothy Keane, Kansas State University, July 15, 2006.

10. Those who deny any utility to the Rosgen classification system tend to be basic researchers who do not favor classification in any form, people with the time to work from the raw data.

11. Regional curves are based on the hydraulic geometry relations described by Luna Leopold and other USGS staff in their seminal 1950s publications (e.g., Leopold and Maddock 1953).

12. In his chapter for the NRCS *Stream Restoration Design* handbook, for example, Rosgen refers to the structures as "stabilization/fish habitat enhancement measures" (Natural Resources Conservation Service 2007, 11-53).

13. Author interview with Dr. Brian Bledsoe, Colorado State University, September 21, 2006. Bledsoe monitored the Three Forks Ranch project from 2001 to 2006.

CHAPTER THREE. *The History of Stream Restoration and the Rise of Rosgen*

1. Unless otherwise noted, the material in this section is drawn from conversations with Rosgen in August 2003 at the NCED/NRC conference in Minneapolis; his Level I short course in Santa Cruz, California, in January 2005; his Level II short course in Fayetteville, Arkansas, in November 2006; and a formal interview on April 22, 2007.

2. Thompson and Stull wrote a very useful history of early stream restoration work in the United States (2002), but no one has yet written about the history of stream restoration over the last four decades as it became a significant component of American environmentalism and developed into a lucrative market. Thus the remainder of this section depends on two main sources: limited information on stream restoration history from sources focused on other topics (Brookes 1988; Riley 1998; and O'Neill 2006) and interviews focused on the history of the field with founding principals of the earliest restoration consulting firms in the United States and senior federal agency staff (Dr. Philip Williams of Philip Williams & Associates in California; Greg Koonce and Dale Miller of Inter-Fluve, Inc., in the Pacific Northwest; James MacBroom of Milone & MacBroom in the Northeast; Robbin Sotir of Sotir & Associates in the Southeast; Dr. Craig Fischenich of the US Army Corps of Engineers Engineer Research and Development Center; and Dr. F. Douglas Shields of the National Sedimentation Laboratory).

3. http://www.usbr.gov/main/about/, accessed August 1, 2011.

4. Wild and Scenic Rivers Act, Pub. L. No. 90-542.

5. The backdrop to the growth of the stream restoration consulting industry is, of course, the development of the environmental consulting industry as a whole. Unfortunately, no one has written a history of environmental consulting, nor are there any sources I could find on current or former numbers of environmental consultants. There are a number of sources with generic statements that the National Association of Environmental Professionals (NAEP) catalyzed the growth of the industry (see, e.g., Hanson 1976, 627; Nelkin 1976, 39; 1977, 31; and Todd 1980, 61), but these authors do not

provide much in the way of supporting evidence. One indicator is that the NAEP started in 1975 and began a certification program in 1979.

6. Author interview with Dr. James MacBroom, Milone & MacBroom, July 24, 2006.

7. Because the National Oceanic and Atmospheric Administration did not allow NRSS to make its data public, this graph does not include approximately nineteen thousand projects from the NRSS database; however, when these projects are added, the trend of exponential growth is still clearly present.

8. Section 404 of the Clean Water Act regulates the discharge of dredged or fill materials into "waters of the United States," which include riparian systems. To do so legally requires a permit from the US Army Corps of Engineers. Any proposed dredging or filling of an existing stream must be shown to be the least environmentally damaging practicable alternative for achieving the overall project purpose. Should significant environmental degradation still result, permit applicants must compensate for their impacts by restoring comparable streams on- or off-site or by purchasing credits from stream mitigation banks that restore streams on a speculative basis, creating a strong incentive to develop stream restoration technologies.

9. For example, according to a 2007 report by the Environmental Law Institute, the federal government alone spent more than $2.9 billion on compensatory mitigation projects required by Clean Water Act permits in 2006. Most likely, the majority of the funds were for wetlands restoration, but even if only one-fourth of the $2.9 billion was spent on streams, this would still indicate a large rise in overall spending on stream restoration in the United States, since many restoration projects are financed by private developers.

10. The 1986 Flood Control Act, section 1135, started the US Army Corps of Engineers restoration program (although it wasn't until four years later that the 1990 Flood Control Act made it a permanent program). In 1989 Lt. Gen. Henry J. Hatch, then commander of the US Army Corps of Engineers, went so far as to hold a press conference announcing that the Corps had to embrace environmental concerns (O'Neill 2006).

11. Data in this section are drawn primarily from separate rounds of semistructured and structured interviews I conducted in 2006 and 2007 (see the appendix for a list of all the interview questions and subjects).

12. Author interview with Dr. Brian Bledsoe, Colorado State University, August 23, 2006.

13. Author interview with Angela Greene, Natural Resources Conservation Service/Canaan Valley Institute, November 17, 2006.

14. Resource Conservation and Development Councils function something like Soil and Water Conservation Districts but on a larger, multicounty scale. They are voluntary associations created to promote linked goals of resource conservation and community development and are linked with the Natural Resources Conservation Service for technical assistance, training, and sometimes funding.

15. Author interview with Dr. Brian Bledsoe, Colorado State University, August 23, 2006.

16. Author interview with Allan Walker, Natural Resources Conservation Service, December 18, 2007.

17. Author interview with Will Harman, principal, Buck Engineering (now principal of Stream Mechanics), August 14, 2006.

18. North Carolina State is to my knowledge the only R1 university that actively supports Natural Channel Design (through its Stream Restoration Program). It is important to note, however, that that support is primarily through the state agricultural extension program, not the university itself.

19. Author interview with Dr. Greg Jennings, North Carolina State University, July 21, 2006.

20. Author interview with David Phlegar, City of Greensboro, North Carolina, November 19, 2007.

21. Author interview with a US Forest Service hydrologist, June 2, 2004.

22. Ibid.

23. Author interview with John Potyondy, US Forest Service, April 29, 2004.

24. Author interview with Dr. Gary Parker, University of Illinois, June 26, 2006.

25. Author interview with Dr. Daniel Levish, US Bureau of Reclamation, June 28, 2006.

CHAPTER FOUR. *Capital Conflicts*

1. For a discussion of twenty-one of the most common critiques, see Lave (2008).

2. In an interview on April 22, 2007, Rosgen showed me a sheet of notes speculating about how to do a broad study, but to my knowledge he has not tried to start such a project.

3. The lowest claim I have seen comes from Mondry, Melia, and Haupt (2006), who report a stability rate of 74 percent for Rosgen structures installed by the North Carolina Ecosystem Enhancement Project in restoration projects two to five years old.

4. Author interview with Will Harman, principal, Buck Engineering (now principal of Stream Mechanics), August 14, 2006.

5. Author interview with Dr. Daniel Levish, US Bureau of Reclamation, June 28, 2006.

6. Author interview with Karin Boyd, principal, Applied Geomorphology, Inc., July 18, 2006.

7. Author interview with Scott Gillilan, principal, Gillilan Associates, Inc., August 10, 2006.

8. Author interview with Dr. David Rosgen, principal, Wildland Hydrology, April 22, 2007.

9. Author interview with Kris Vyverberg, California Department of Fish and Game, June 3, 2004.

10. Shared methods include Wolman pebble counts, which are critical to determining channel classification and also ubiquitous among Rosgen's critics (though disagree-

ments about where the active bed ends and the bank begins mean that their sampling methodologies vary). And while perhaps not as commonly used by Rosgen's critics as by his supporters, scour chains and bank pins are accepted methods of measuring short-term erosion in both camps.

11. Author interview with Dr. F. Douglas Shields, Agricultural Research Service (ARS) National Sedimentation Laboratory, June 13, 2006.

12. Author interview with James MacBroom, principal, Milone & MacBroom, July 24, 2006.

13. Author interview with Kris Vyverberg, California Department of Fish and Game, June 3, 2004.

14. Conversations with Dr. David Rosgen, 2007 and 2009, and author interview with Dr. Brian Bledsoe, Colorado State University, August 23, 2006.

15. Author interview with MacBroom, July 24, 2006.

16. Author interview with Steve Gough, principal, Little River Consulting, June 19, 2006.

17. Author interview with Dr. Gary Parker, University of Illinois, June 26, 2006.

18. Author interview with Dr. Daniel Levish, US Bureau of Reclamation, June 28, 2006.

19. Hey is the instructor for the alternative Level I course, Fluvial Geomorphology for Engineers, the only Rosgen short course taught by someone other than Rosgen. It is worth noting, however, that the British PhD system requires two outside examiners to sign off on any degree, so Hey's employment status is much less relevant than it would be in the US system.

20. Only the most vehement critics put it this bluntly, but even moderate critics sometimes point to Rosgen's lack of formal credentials obliquely or even unconsciously. Dr. Gary Parker, for example, who seems to be one of the most Rosgen-supportive members of the process research community, made the following comment: "I hope you have a chance to talk with Eric [Larsen], because he did learn as an apprentice to Rosgen . . . [and] then went on to get a very solid background in engineering and river geomorphology." The implication is that an apprenticeship with Rosgen would not in and of itself provide such a background.

21. To their credit, some university- and agency-based scientists are trying to communicate this cultural rift to him. One of Rosgen's most vehement critics, Andrew Simon of the National Sedimentation Laboratory, reports saying this to him: "You need to get yourself out there and not just in conference proceedings. You need to write yourself up in the journals. Not so that you can put something after your name, but because this is how science moves, this is how it *works*. This is how you get to look at my work and critique and review it. And this is how I get to look at your work and critique and review it. That's how we learn and move forward" (author interview with Simon, December 13, 2006). Taking this further, Rollin Hotchkiss, a hydraulic engineer at Brigham Young University and the current editor of the *Journal of Hydraulic Engineering*, has been actively working with Rosgen to help him publish his work.

22. See, for example, http://www.asce.org/reportcard/2009/grades.cfm.

23. Author interview with John Potyondy, USFS, April 29, 2004.

24. Author interview with Dr. David Rosgen, Wildland Hydrology, April 22, 2007.

25. In the Level I course I attended, just under a third of people had previous restoration experience, but that may have been atypical.

26. Author interview with Rosgen, April 22, 2007.

27. In effect, we use flooding as an instrument of primitive accumulation. For example, in Saint Louis more than twenty-eight thousand houses and thousands of acres of commercial development, worth approximately $2.2 billion, have been built on parts of the Mississippi River floodplain that were underwater during the 1993 floods (Saulny 2007).

28. For example, Peter Wilcock, a sediment transport researcher at Johns Hopkins University, explained that he has not spoken publicly about his concerns with Rosgen's sediment transport work for the EPA because he has not been able to find out enough about it to confirm or deny his concerns: "I have been careful not to publicly criticize his design methods because some of his more vocal defenders complain, I think correctly, that there are lots of people who complain about Dave's methods without actually having learned what they are. Most of us who are professionals in this learn what other people's methods are by reading about them in the scientific literature, not by taking courses on them. And so that information is not available [to us]" (author interview with Dr. Peter Wilcock, Johns Hopkins University, July 24, 2006).

29. Author interview with Dr. David Montgomery, University of Washington, June 28, 2006.

30. Author interview with Dr. Andrew Simon, ARS National Sedimentation Laboratory, December 13, 2006.

31. Author interview with Dr. Craig Fischenich, US Army Corps of Engineers Waterways Experiment Station, June 27, 2006.

32. The authors maintain the quotes around the phrase Natural Channel Design throughout the paper to underline their contestation of that label.

33. According to lead author Peter Wilcock, the NCED primary investigator for stream restoration, this curriculum and certification effort fizzled out. The NCED recently restarted the conversation in its national newsletter. It is not yet clear whether the process can establish sufficient momentum to produce a viable national curriculum and certification process.

CHAPTER FIVE. *Building a Base of Support*

1. Author interview with Steven Gough, principal, Little River Consulting, June 19, 2006.

2. Author interview with Laura Wildman, American Rivers, June 4, 2004.

3. Author interview with Dr. Ann Riley, State Water Quality Control Board, June 19, 2006.

4. I know of two: North Carolina State University, and California Polytechnic San Louis Obispo. West Virginia University taught the design approach during summer short courses from 2002 until 2004.

5. Information provided by Wildland Hydrology.

6. A recently added fifth course deals with the nuts and bolts of the construction process, and there is also an alternative first course for people with engineering degrees, who are assumed to need a different introduction to restoration.

7. Estimating the proportion of participants in the stream restoration field with Rosgen training is an imprecise business. We know from figures kept by Wildland Hydrology, Rosgen's consulting firm, that as of 2006 over ten thousand unique students had attended his Level I, II, III, or IV course. This number does not include students who took special courses contracted for by specific agencies. The EPA, for example, used to organize Rosgen courses just for its staff. Wildland Hydrology does not track these numbers.

Estimating the total number of restoration practitioners in the United States is even less precise. There is no professional organization of stream restoration practitioners to ask about membership numbers. Nor is there a national conference devoted solely to stream restoration to query about attendance or a single journal read by the majority of stream restoration participants to ask about circulation figures. As a proxy, three of the major conferences that stream restoration researchers and practitioners attend are (1) River Restoration NorthWest (RRNW), (2) the North Carolina Stream Restoration Program Southeast Regional Conference (NC SRC), and (3) the American Society of Civil Engineers' Environmental and Water Resources Institute (EWRI) conference, which includes a substantial restoration-related strand of presentations. In 2006 approximately 263 people attended RRNW, approximately 500 people attended the SRP biennial conference, and 778 people attended the annual EWRI conference for a total of 1,541 conference attendees. Ignoring the fact that many people attending the EWRI conference are not involved in stream restoration and the possibility of overlapping attendance among these conferences in order to maximize the potential number of participants, and assuming that only one in ten participants in the restoration community attends such conferences in any given year, there would have been somewhere on the order of fifteen thousand restoration field participants in the United States in 2006. Thus a conservative, though very rough, estimate would be that approximately two-thirds of the stream restoration community in the United States has been through at least one of Rosgen's courses.

8. My favorite of these stories comes from an agency staff person who watched with mounting disbelief as employees of an NCD consulting firm stopped to put on white cowboy hats before photographing each of the cross sections they surveyed.

9. Author interview with Angela Greene, NRCS and Canaan Valley Institute, November 17, 2006.

10. Author interview with Cheryl Harrelson, principal, Steady Stream Hydrology, August 30, 2006.

11. In the Level I course, students receive *Applied River Morphology*, Rosgen's 1996

textbook on classifying streams and valley types. In the Level II course, students are given Rosgen's *Field Guide for Stream Classification*, a lightweight, waterproof, Cliff Notes version of *Applied River Morphology* intended to be carried into the field. Both of these texts are self-published. In the Level I course, students are also given a second bound manual with supporting materials for the lectures as well as Rosgen's *Catena* paper, the Blanco River case study from the 1992 NRC report, and a number of Rosgen's conference papers.

12. In the first course, students are given copies of a textbook that Kondolf edited with Hervé Piégay, *Tools in Fluvial Geomorphology*. Rather than being a focused discussion of the material presented in course lectures, as Rosgen's textbook is, this text is a compendium of chapters about different measurement techniques, some of which were covered in course lectures but most of which were not. At the end of the first course, the instructors also distributed a compact disc with key scientific papers referred to in lectures, but this was clearly an afterthought, as the CDs were produced in the classroom on the last day of the course by a TA (me) while students were presenting their work.

13. As Scott McBain, an academically trained restoration consultant in northern California, said when asked whether he uses hydraulic geometry: "I use it just for checking what we're doing, but I don't design from it." Author interview with Scott McBain, principal, McBain & Trush, July 17, 2006.

14. Author interview with Dr. David Rosgen, Wildland Hydrology, April 22, 2007.

15. Data provided by Lael Gilbert for the two Utah State courses, Laura Craig for the Maryland course, and Shannah Anderson for the California course.

16. Author interview with Dr. Vaughan Voller, University of Minnesota, September 19, 2006.

17. Author interview with Syd Brown, California Department of Parks and Recreation, June 24, 2004.

18. Author interview with Dr. Timothy Keane, Kansas State University, July 15, 2006.

19. Author interview with Dr. David Montgomery, University of Washington, June 28, 2006.

20. Bourdieu writes: "The field of argument which orthodoxy and heterodoxy define by their struggles is demarcated against the background of the field of *doxa*, the aggregate of presuppositions which the antagonists regard as self-evident and outside the area of argument because they constitute the tacit condition of argument" (1975, 34).

21. Author interview with Steve Gough, principal, Little River Consulting, June 19, 2006.

CHAPTER SIX. *The Political Economy of Stream Restoration*

1. Although at one point he wrote that the forces at work at the heteronomous end of a field are typically not economic (Bourdieu 1998), in *The Rules of Art*, his most extended field analysis, Bourdieu repeatedly equated heteronomy with economic capital and influence by market forces (1996a, 83, 114, 115, 120–21, 141).

2. The critics were Matt Kondolf of the University of California, Berkeley, and Andrew

Simon of the Agricultural Research Service's National Sedimentation Laboratory, a branch of the US Department of Agriculture.

3. NSF lists no grants for stream or river restoration before 1990. I searched using the phrases "stream restoration" and "river restoration." The value of NSF grants awarded in 2002 was actually almost $25 million, $23.2 million of which went to fund the National Center for Earth-Surface Dynamics (NCED) at the University of Minnesota. However, stream restoration is only one of NCED's three foci, so presumably the amount dedicated to it has been much less than the total.

4. Author interview with Dr. Peter Wilcock, Johns Hopkins University, July 24, 2006.

5. Author interview with Dr. Martin Doyle, Duke University, June 15, 2006.

6. Author interview with Dr. Steven Kite, West Virginia University, July 26, 2006.

7. Author interview with Dr. Gary Parker, University of Illinois, June 26, 2006.

8. Conversation with Dr. Jack Schmidt, Utah State University, October 22, 2004.

9. Recent studies show that while stream mitigation projects reached targeted geomorphic success criteria, none reached minimum success criteria based on benthic macroinvertebrate communities (Violin et al. 2011) or nutrient retention (Sudduth et al. 2011).

10. The only place I found in Bourdieu's work on fields where he entertains this possibility even for a moment is in his book *The State Nobility*, where in the midst of an almost Gramscian take on the ways in which the dominated can benefit from conflict among the dominant he says: "The dominated can always take advantage of or benefit from conflicts among the powerful, who, quite often, need their cooperation in order to triumph in these conflicts" (Bourdieu 1996b, 389). Unfortunately, he does not elaborate on this potential.

CHAPTER SEVEN. *Conclusions*

1. Author interview with Dr. Martin Doyle, Duke University, June 15, 2006.

2. Author interview with Dr. Gary Parker, University of Illinois at Urbana-Champaign, June 26, 2006.

3. Author interview with Dr. Martin Doyle, Duke University, June 15, 2006.

4. One symptom of this more nuanced view is that when National River Restoration Science Synthesis (NRSS) researchers asked project managers in the Southeast (the majority of whom were in North Carolina) about the success of projects, 60 percent said "partially," a striking contrast with the national average of 65 percent "completely" successful. This difference may be a result of the high rate of project monitoring in North Carolina, which gives the restoration community there an unusually deep knowledge of what works and doesn't work about restoration projects. See Sudduth, Meyer, and Bernhardt (2007, 580–82) for more details.

5. Author interview with William Harman, Buck Engineering/Michael Baker Corporation, August 14, 2006. In a follow-up e-mail, Harman noted that reference reaches are not their only or even their primary source for designing new channels:

"We use the reference reach as one approach for developing design criteria. We also use monitoring results from past projects, computer models, and equations from the literature. We use different techniques depending on the type of project and look for converging lines of evidence. It's about applying the right solution to the right problem." Clearly, this is not a case of mindless application of the NCD approach.

6. Author interview with Richard Everhart, NRCS/Surry County Soil and Water Conservation District, November 30, 2007.

REFERENCES

Adas, Michael. 1989. *Machines as the Measure of Men: Science, Technology, and Ideologies of Western Dominance.* Ithaca, N.Y.: Cornell University Press.

Arthur, M. B. 1936. *Fish Stream Improvement Handbook.* Washington, D.C.: US Forest Service.

Ashmore, Peter. 1999. "What Would We Do without Rosgen? Rational Regime Relations and Natural Channels." Paper read at the Second International Conference on Natural Systems Design, Niagara Falls, Canada.

Asner, Glen. 2004. "The Linear Model, the U.S. Department of Defense, and the Golden Age of Industrial Research." In *The Science-Industry Nexus*, edited by K. Grandin, N. Wormbs, and S. Widmalm, 3–30. Sagamore Beach, Mass.: Science History Publications.

———. 2006. "The Cold War and American Industrial Research." PhD diss., Carnegie Mellon University.

Bakker, Karen. 2005. "Neoliberalizing Nature? Market Environmentalism in Water Supply in England and Wales." *Annals of the Association of American Geographers* 95(3): 542–65.

Bavington, Dean. 2010. *Managed Annihilation: An Unnatural History of the Newfoundland Cod Collapse.* Vancouver: University of British Columbia Press.

Beck, Ulrich. 1992. *Risk Society: Towards a New Modernity.* Thousand Oaks, Calif.: Sage Publications.

Bellamy Foster, John. 2002. *Ecology against Capitalism.* New York: Monthly Review Press.

Bernhardt, E. S., M. A. Palmer, J. D. Allan, G. Alexander, K. Barnas, S. Brooks, J. Carr, S. Clayton, C. Dahm, J. Follstad-Shah, D. Galat, S. Gloss, P. Goodwin, D. Hart, B. Hassett, R. Jenkinson, S. Katz, G. M. Kondolf, P. S. Lake, R. Lave, J. L. Meyer, T. K. O'Donnell, L. Pagano, B. Powell, and E. Sudduth. 2005. "Synthesizing U.S. River Restoration Efforts." *Science* 308:636–37.

Blaikie, Piers. 1985. *The Political Economy of Soil Erosion in Developing Countries.* New York: John Wiley & Sons.

———. 1999. "A Review of Political Ecology." *Zeitschrift für Wirtschaftsgeographie* 43(3–4): 131–47.

Blaikie, Piers, and Harold Brookfield. 1987. *Land Degradation and Society.* London: Methuen.

Bourdieu, Pierre. 1975. "The Specificity of the Scientific Field and the Social Conditions of the Progress of Reason." *Social Science Information* 14(6): 19–47.

———. 1983. "The Field of Cultural Production, or: The Economic World Reversed." *Poetics* 12:311–56.

———. 1991. "Genesis and Structure of the Religious Field." In *Comparative Social Research: Religious Institutions*, edited by Craig Calhoun, 1–44. Greenwich, Conn.: Jai Press.

———. 1996a. *The Rules of Art: Genesis and Structure of the Literary Field*. Translated by Susan Emanuel. Stanford, Calif.: Stanford University Press.

———. 1996b. *The State Nobility: Elite Schools in the Field of Power*. Translated by Lauretta C. Clough. Stanford, Calif.: Stanford University Press.

———. 1998. "Rethinking the State: Genesis and Structure of the Bureaucratic Field." In *Practical Reason: On the Theory of Action*, edited by Pierre Bourdieu, 35–63. Stanford, Calif.: Stanford University Press. Originally published in *Sociological Theory* (1994).

Bourdieu, Pierre, and Loic J. D. Wacquant. 1992. *An Invitation to Reflexive Sociology*. Chicago: University of Chicago Press.

Bourdieu, Pierre, Loic J. D. Wacquant, and Samar Farage. 1994. "Rethinking the State: Genesis and Structure of the Bureaucratic Field." *Sociological Theory* 12(1): 1–18.

Bowker, Geoffrey C., and Susan Leigh Star. 1999. *Sorting Things Out: Classification and Its Consequences*. Cambridge, Mass.: MIT Press.

Braun, Bruce. 2002. *The Intemperate Rainforest: Nature, Culture and Power on Canada's West Coast*. Minneapolis: University of Minnesota Press.

Braun, Bruce, and Noel Castree. 1998. "The Construction of Nature and the Nature of Construction: Analytical and Political Tools for Building Survivable Futures." In *Remaking Reality: Nature at the Millennium*, edited by Bruce Braun and Noel Castree, 3–42. New York: Routledge.

Brookes, A. 1988. *Channelized Rivers: Perspectives for Environmental Management*. Chichester: John Wiley & Sons.

Canaan, Joyce E., and Wesley Shumar. 2008. *Structure and Agency in the Neoliberal University*. New York: Routledge.

Castree, Noel. 2008. "Neoliberalising Nature: The Logics of Deregulation and Reregulation." *Environment and Planning A* 40:131–52.

———. 2010. "Neoliberalism and the Biophysical Environment: A Synthesis and Evaluation of Research." *Environment and Society* no. 1:5–45.

Cooper, Melinda. 2010. "Turbulent Worlds: Between Financial and Environmental Crisis." *Theory, Culture, and Society* 27(2–3): 167–90.

Crosby, Alfred W. 1986. *Ecological Imperialism: The Biological Expansion of Europe, 900–1900*. Cambridge: Cambridge University Press.

Davis, Diana K. 2007. *Resurrecting the Granary of Rome: Environmental History and French Colonial Expansion in North Africa*. Athens: Ohio University Press.

Demeritt, David. 1998. "Science, Social Constructivism and Nature." In *Remaking Reality: Nature at the Millennium*, edited by Bruce Braun and Noel Castree, 173–93. New York: Routledge.

Doyle, Martin W., and Jon M. Harbor. 2000. "Discussion of 'Evaluation of Rosgen's Streambank Erosion Potential Assessment in Northeast Oklahoma' by Harmel." *Journal of the American Water Resources Association* 36(5): 1191–92.

Doyle, Martin W., Dale E. Miller, and Jon M. Harbor. 1999. "Should River Restoration Be Based on Classification Schemes or Process Models? Insights from the History of Geomorphology." Paper read at the ASCE International Conference on Water Resources Engineering, Seattle, Wash.

Doyle, Martin W., F. Douglas Shields, Karin F. Boyd, Peter B. Skidmore, and DeWitt Dominick. 2007. "Channel-Forming Discharge Selection in River Restoration Design." *Journal of Hydraulic Engineering* 133(7): 831–37.

Dunne, Thomas, and Luna B. Leopold. 1978. *Water in Environmental Planning.* New York: W. H. Freeman and Company.

Duvall, Chris. 2011. "Ferricrete, Forests, and Temporal Scale in the Production of Colonial Science in Africa." In *Knowing Nature: Conversations at the Border of Political Ecology and Science Studies,* edited by Mara Goldman, Paul Nadasdy, and Matt Turner, 113–27. Chicago: University of Chicago Press.

Egan, David. 1990. "Historic Initiatives in Ecological Restoration." *Restoration & Management Notes* 8(2): 83–89.

Environmental Law Institute. 2007. *Mitigation of Impacts to Fish and Wildlife Habitat: Estimating Costs and Identifying Opportunities.*

Epstein, Steven. 1996. *Impure Science: Aids, Activism, and the Politics of Knowledge.* Berkeley: University of California Press.

Espeland, Wendy. 1998. *The Struggle for Water: Politics, Rationality, and Identity in the American Southwest.* Chicago: University of Chicago Press.

Evans, James. 2010. "Industry Collaboration and Secrecy in Academic Science." *Social Studies of Science* 40(5): 757–91.

Fairhead, James, and Melissa Leach. 1996. *Misreading the African Landscape: Society and Ecology in a Forest-Savanna Mosaic.* Cambridge: Cambridge University Press.

———. 2003. *Science, Society and Power: Environmental Knowledge and Policy in West Africa and the Caribbean.* Cambridge: Cambridge University Press.

Federal Interagency Stream Restoration Working Group. 1998. *Stream Corridor Restoration: Principles, Processes, and Practices.* Washington, D.C.

Fisher, Jill A. 2009. *Medical Research for Hire: The Political Economy of Pharmaceutical Clinical Trials.* New Brunswick, N.J.: Rutgers University Press.

Forsyth, Tim. 2003. *Critical Political Ecology: The Politics of Environmental Science.* London: Routledge.

Geiger, Roger, and Creso Sa. 2008. *Tapping the Riches of Science: Universities and the Promise of Economic Growth.* Cambridge, Mass.: Harvard University Press.

Gibbons, Michael, Camille Limoges, Helga Nowotny, Simon Schwartzman, Peter Scott, and Martin Trow. 1994. *The New Production of Knowledge: The Dynamics of Science and Research in Contemporary Societies.* London: Sage.

Gillilan, Scott. 1996. "Use and Misuse of Channel Classification Schemes." *Stream Notes*, October, 2–3.

Goldman, Mara, and Matthew D. Turner. 2011. Introduction to *Knowing Nature: Conversations at the Intersection of Political Ecology and Science Studies*, edited by Mara Goldman, Paul Nadasdy, and Matthew D. Turner, 1–23. Chicago: University of Chicago Press.

Goldman, Michael. 2004. "Imperial Science, Imperial Nature: Environmental Knowledge for the World (Bank)." In *Earthly Politics: Local and Global in Environmental Governance*, edited by Sheila Jasanoff and Marybeth Long Martello, 55–80. Cambridge, Mass.: MIT Press.

———. 2005. *Imperial Nature: The World Bank and Struggles for Social Justice in the Age of Globalization*. New Haven, Conn.: Yale University Press.

Gordon, Nancy. 1995. "Summary of Technical Testimony in the Colorado Water Division 1 Trial." US Forest Service.

Gould, Stephen Jay. 2000. "Deconstructing the 'Science Wars' by Reconstructing an Old Mold." *Science* 287:253–61.

Greenberg, Daniel. 2007. *Science for Sale*. Chicago: University of Chicago Press.

Hall, Marcus. 2005. *Earth Repair: A Transatlantic History of Environmental Restoration*. Charlottesville: University of Virginia Press.

Hanson, Charles H. 1976. "Ethics in the Business of Science." *Ecology* 57(4): 627–28.

Haraway, Donna. 1989. *Primate Visions: Gender, Race and Nature in the World of Modern Science*. New York: Routledge.

Harvey, David. 2005. *A Brief History of Neoliberalism*. Oxford: Oxford University Press.

Heatherman, William. 2005. Re: Rosgen and Professional Ethics Discussion. E-mail to the American Society of Civil Engineers' River Restoration Committee, September 2.

Hecht, Gabrielle. 2002. "Rupture-Talk in the Nuclear Age: Conjugating Colonial Power in Africa." *Social Studies of Science* 32(5–6): 691–728.

Hecht, Susanna. 1985. "Environment, Development and Politics: Capital Accumulation and the Livestock Sector in Eastern Amazonia." *World Development* 13(6): 663–84.

Hilgartner, Stephen. 2000. *Science on Stage — Expert Advice as Public Drama*. Stanford, Calif.: Stanford University Press.

Jasanoff, Sheila. 1990. *The Fifth Branch: Science Advisors as Policymakers*. Cambridge, Mass.: Harvard University Press.

Jasanoff, Sheila, and Marybeth Long Martello. 2004. *Earthly Politics: Local and Global in Environmental Governance*. Cambridge, Mass.: MIT Press.

Jordan, William R., III. 2000. "Restoration, Community, and Wilderness." In *Restoring Nature: Perspectives from the Social Sciences and Humanities*, edited by Paul H. Gobster and R. Bruce Hull, 21–36. Washington, D.C.: Island Press.

Juracek, Kyle E., and Faith A. Fitzpatrick. 2003. "Limitations and Implications of

Stream Classification." *Journal of the American Water Resources Association* 39(3): 659–70.

Knighton, David. 1984. *Fluvial Forms and Process*. London: Edward Arnold.

Knorr-Cetina, Karin. 1981. *The Manufacture of Knowledge: An Essay on the Constructivist and Contextual Nature of Science*. Oxford: Pergamon Press.

Kohler, Robert E. 2002. *Landscapes & Labscapes: Exploring the Lab-Field Border in Biology*. Chicago: University of Chicago Press.

Kondolf, G. Mathias. 1995. "Geomorphological Stream Channel Classification in Aquatic Habitat Restoration: Uses and Limitations." *Aquatic Conservation: Marine and Freshwater Ecosystems* 5:127–41.

———. 1998. "Lessons Learned from River Restoration Projects in California." *Aquatic Conservation: Marine and Freshwater Ecosystems* 8:39–52.

———. 2007. "River Restoration in North America: Meandering Channels for All?" Paper read at the Association of American Geographers, San Francisco.

Kondolf, G. Mathias, M. W. Smeltzer, and S. Railsback. 2001. "Design and Performance of a Channel Reconstruction Project in a Coastal California Gravel-Bed Stream." *Environmental Management* 28(6): 761–76.

Latour, Bruno. 1987. *Science in Action: How to Follow Scientists and Engineers through Society*. Cambridge, Mass.: Harvard University Press.

———. 1999. *Pandora's Hope: Essays on the Reality of Science Studies*. Cambridge, Mass.: Harvard University Press.

———. 2005. *Reassembling the Social: An Introduction to Actor-Network Theory*. Oxford: Oxford University Press.

Latour, Bruno, and Steven Woolgar. 1986. *Laboratory Life: The Social Construction of Scientific Facts*. Princeton, N.J.: Princeton University Press.

Lave, Rebecca. 2008. "The Rosgen Wars and the Shifting Construction of Scientific Expertise." PhD diss., University of California at Berkeley.

Lave, Rebecca, Martin W. Doyle, and Morgan M. Robertson. 2010. "Privatizing Stream Restoration in the U.S." *Social Studies of Science* 40(5): 677–703.

Lave, Rebecca, Philip Mirowski, and Samuel Randalls. 2010. "Introduction: STS and Neoliberal Science." *Social Studies of Science* 40(5): 659–75.

Lave, Rebecca, Morgan M. Robertson, and Martin W. Doyle. 2008. "Why You Should Pay Attention to Stream Mitigation Banking." *Ecological Restoration* 26(4): 287–89.

Lawless, Christopher, and Robin Williams. 2010. "Helping with Inquiries, or Helping with Profits? The Trials and Tribulations of a Technology of Forensic Reasoning." *Social Studies of Science* 40(5): 731–55.

Leopold, Luna B., and T. Maddock. 1953. *The Hydraulic Geometry of Stream Channels and Some Physiological Implications*. Washington, D.C.: US Geological Survey.

Mansfield, Becky. 2004. "Rules of Privatization: Contradictions in Neoliberal Regulation of North Pacific Fisheries." *Annals of the Association of American Geographers* 94(3): 565–84.

Mavhunga, Clapperton. 2011. "Vermin Beings: On Pestiferous Animals and Human Game." *Social Text* 29(106): 151–76.

McCarthy, James, and W. Scott Prudham. 2004. "Neoliberal Nature and the Nature of Neoliberalism." *Geoforum* 35:275–83.

Miller, Dale E., Peter B. Skidmore, and Dale J. White. 2001. "Channel Design." Washington Department of Fish and Wildlife, Washington Department of Ecology, Washington Department of Transportation.

Miller, J. R., and R. C. Kochel. 2008. "Assessment of Channel Dynamics and Its Implications to Effective Channel Design." Paper read at the North Carolina State Stream Restoration Institute.

Miller, Jerry R., and John B. Ritter. 1996. "An Examination of the Rosgen Classification of Natural Rivers." *Catena* 27:295–99.

Mirowski, Philip. 2009. "Postface: Defining Neoliberalism." In *The Road from Mount Pelerin: The Making of the Neoliberal Thought Collective*, edited by Philip Mirowski and Dieter Plehwe, 417–55. Cambridge, Mass.: Harvard University Press.

———. 2011. *Science-Mart: Privatizing American Science*. Cambridge, Mass.: Harvard University Press.

Mirowski, Philip, and Dieter Plehwe, eds. 2009. *The Road from Mount Pelerin: The Making of the Neoliberal Thought Collective*. Cambridge, Mass.: Harvard University Press.

Mondry, Zackary, Greg Melia, and Mac Haupt. 2006. "Stability of Engineered Stream Structures in North Carolina Restoration Projects." North Carolina Ecosystem Enhancement Program. http://www.bae.ncsu.edu/programs/extension/wqg /sri/2006conference/presentations.html.

Montgomery, James A. 2000. "The Use of Natural Resource Information in Wetland Ecosystem Creation and Restoration: Reflections on the Value of Talking and Listening." *Ecological Restoration* 18(1): 45–50.

National Research Council (NRC). 1992. *Restoration of Aquatic Ecosystems: Science, Technology, and Public Policy*. Washington, D.C.: National Academy Press.

Natural Resources Conservation Service (NRCS). 2007. *Stream Restoration Design*. National Engineering Handbook, pt. 654. LANDCARE. Des Moines, Iowa: US Department of Agriculture.

Nedeva, Maria, and Rebecca Boden. 2006. "Changing Science: The Advent of Neoliberalism." *Prometheus* 24(3): 269–81.

Nelkin, Dorothy. 1976. "Ecologists and the Public Interest." *Hastings Center Report* 6(1): 38–44.

———. 1977. "Scientists and Professional Responsibility: The Experience of American Ecologists." *Social Studies of Science* 7(1): 75–95.

Newfield, Christopher. 2008. *Unmaking the Public University*. Cambridge, Mass.: Harvard University Press.

Nowotny, H., and M. Gibbons. 2001. *Rethinking Science: Knowledge and the Public in an Age of Uncertainty*. Cambridge: Polity Press.

Nowotny, H., D. Pestre, E. Schmidt-Assman, H. Schultze-Fielitz, and H. Trute. 2005. *The Public Nature of Science under Assault*. Berlin: Springer.

O'Neill, Karen M. 2006. *Rivers by Design: State Power and the Origins of U.S. Flood Control*. Durham, N.C.: Duke University Press.

Ong, Elisa K., and Stanton A. Glantz. 2001. "Constructing 'Sound Science' and 'Good Epidemiology': Tobacco, Lawyers, and Public Relations Firms." *American Journal of Public Health* 91(11): 1749–57.

Palmer, M. A., and S. Filoso. 2009. "The Restoration of Ecosystems for Environmental Markets." *Science* 325(5,940): 575–76.

Palmer, Margaret A., Richard F. Ambrose, and N. LeRoy Poff. 1997. "Ecological Theory and Community Restoration Ecology." *Restoration Ecology* 5:291–300.

Peck, Jamie, and Adam Tickell. 2002. "Neoliberalizing Space." *Antipode* 34(3): 380–404.

Peet, Richard, Paul Robbins, and Michael Watts. 2011. *Global Political Ecology*. London: Routledge.

Peet, Richard, and Michael Watts. 1996. *Liberation Ecologies: Environment, Development, Social Movements*. 1st ed. London: Routledge.

———. 2004. *Liberation Ecologies: Environment, Development, Social Movements*. 2nd ed. London: Routledge.

Peluso, Nancy. 1992. *Rich Forests, Poor People: Resource Control and Resistance in Java*. Berkeley: University of California Press.

———. 1993. "Coercing Conservation? The Politics of State Resource Control." *Global Environmental Change* 3(2): 199–218.

Peluso, Nancy, and Michael Watts. 2001. *Violent Environments*. Ithaca, N.Y.: Cornell University Press.

Pestre, Dominique. 2003. "Regimes of Knowledge Production in Society: Towards a More Political and Social Reading." *Minerva* 41:245–61.

———. 2005. "The Technosciences between Markets, Social Worries and the Political: How to Imagine a Better Future?" In *The Public Nature of Science under Assault: Politics, Markets, Science and the Law*, edited by Helga Nowotny, Dominique Pestre, Eberhard Schmidt-Assman, Helmuth Schultze-Fielitz, and Hans-Heinrich Trute, 29–52. Berlin: Springer.

Phillips, Jonathan D. 2007. The Perfect Landscape. *Geomorphology* 84(3–4): 159–69.

Porter, Theodore M. 1995. *Trust in Numbers: The Pursuit of Objectivity in Science and Public Life*. Princeton, N.J.: Princeton University Press.

Powell, Walter, Jason Owen-Smith, and Jeanette Colyvas. 2007. "Innovation and Emulation: Lessons from American Universities in Selling Private Rights to Public Knowledge." *Minerva* 45:121–42.

Raffles, Hugh. 2002. *In Amazonia: A Natural History*. Princeton, N.J.: Princeton University Press.

Randalls, Samuel. 2010. "Weather Profits: Weather Derivatives and the Commercialization of Meteorology." *Social Studies of Science* 40(5): 705–30.

Riley, Ann L. 1998. *Restoring Streams in Cities: A Guide for Planners, Policymakers, and Citizens*. Washington, D.C.: Island Press.

Robbins, Paul. 1998. "Authority and Environment: Institutional Landscapes in Rajasthan, India." *Annals of the Association of American Geographers* 88(3): 410–35.

Robertson, Morgan M. 2006. "The Nature that Capital Can See: Science, State and Market in the Commodification of Ecosystem Services." *Environment and Planning D: Society and Space* 24(3): 367–87.

Robertson, Morgan M., Todd BenDor, Rebecca Lave, Adam Riggsbee, J. B. Ruhl, and Martin W. Doyle. In review. "Stacking Ecosystem Services." *Frontiers in Biology*.

Roper, Brett B., John M. Buffington, Eric Archer, Chris Moyer, and Mike Ward. 2008. "The Role of Observer Variation in Determining Rosgen Stream Types in Northeastern Oregon Mountain Streams." *Journal of the American Water Resources Association* 44(2): 417–27.

Rosgen, David L. 1994. "A Classification of Natural Rivers." *Catena* 22(3): 169–99.

———. 1996. *Applied River Morphology*. Pagosa Springs, Colo.: Wildland Hydrology.

———. 2006. "The Natural Channel Design Method for River Restoration." Paper read at the ASCE Environmental & Water Resources Institute, Omaha, Nebr.

———. 2007a. "The Rosgen Geomorphic Approach for Natural Channel Design." In *Stream Restoration Design*. National Engineering Handbook, pt. 654. LANDCARE. Des Moines, Iowa: US Department of Agriculture.

———. 2007b. *Watershed Assessment of River Stability and Sediment Supply*. Fort Collins, Colo.: Wildland Hydrology.

Saulny, S. 2007. "Development Rises on St. Louis Area Flood Plains." *New York Times*, May 15.

Sayre, Nathan F. 2002. *Ranching, Endangered Species, and Urbanization in the Southwest: Species of Capital*. Tucson: University of Arizona Press.

———. 2008. "The Genesis, History, and Limits of Carrying Capacity." *Annals of the Association of American Geographers* 98(1): 120–34.

Sear, D. A. 1994. "River Restoration and Geomorphology." *Aquatic Conservation: Marine and Freshwater Ecosystems* 4:169–77.

Shapin, Steven, and Simon Schaeffer. 1985. *Leviathan and the Air Pump: Hobbes, Boyle and the Experimental Life*. Princeton, N.J.: Princeton University Press.

Shields, F. Douglas, A. Brookes, and Jeffrey P. Haltiner. 1999. "Geomorphological Approaches to Incised Stream Channel Restoration in the United States and Europe." In *Incised River Channels*, edited by Steven Darby and Andrew Simon, 371–94. New York: John Wiley & Sons.

Shields, F. Douglas, and Ronald Copeland. 2006. "Empirical and Analytical Approaches for Stream Channel Design." Paper read at the Federal Interagency Sediment Conference, April 2–6, Reno, Nev.

Shields, F. Douglas, Ronald R. Copeland, Peter C. Klingeman, Martin W. Doyle, and Andrew Simon. 2003. "Design for Stream Restoration." *Journal of Hydraulic Engineering* 129(3): 575–84.

———. 2009. "Chapter 9. Stream Restoration." In *Manual 54 Update*. Reston, Va.: American Society of Civil Engineers.

Simon, Andrew. 2006. "Flow Energy, Time, and Evolution of Dynamic Fluvial Systems: Implications for Stabilization and Restoration of Unstable Systems." Paper read at the World Environmental and Water Resources Congress, May 21–25, Omaha, Nebr.

Simon, Andrew, and Janine Castro. 2003. "Measurement and Analysis of Alluvial Channel Form." In *Tools in Fluvial Geomorphology*, edited by G. M. Kondolf and Hervé Piégay, 291–322. Chichester: John Wiley & Sons.

Simon, Andrew, Martin W. Doyle, G. M. Kondolf, F. Douglas Shields, B. Rhoads, Gordon Grant, Faith A. Fitzpatrick, Kyle E. Juracek, Munsell McPhillips, and James MacBroom. 2005. "How Well Do the Rosgen Classification and Associated 'Natural Channel Design' Methods Integrate and Quantify Fluvial Processes and Channel Response?" Paper read at the ASCE EWRI, Anchorage, Alaska.

Simon, Andrew, Martin W. Doyle, G. M. Kondolf, F. Douglas Shields, B. Rhoads, and Munsell McPhillips. 2007. "Critical Evaluation of How the Rosgen Classification and Associated 'Natural Channel Design' Methods Fail to Integrate and Quantify Fluvial Processes and Channel Response." *Journal of the American Water Resources Association* 43(5): 1–15.

Simon, Andrew, and E. J. Langendoen. 2006. "A Deterministic Bank-Stability and Toe-Erosion Model for Stream Restoration." Paper read at the Environmental and Water Resources Congress, May 21–25, Omaha, Nebr.

Slate, Louise O., F. Douglas Shields, John S. Schwartz, Donald D. Carpenter, and Gary E. Freeman. 2007. "Engineering Design Standards and Liability for Stream Channel Restoration." *Journal of Hydraulic Engineering* 133(10): 1099–1102.

Slaughter, Sheila, and Gary Rhoades. 2002. "The Emergence of a Competitiveness R&D Policy Coalition and the Commercialization of Academic Science." In *Science Bought and Sold*, edited by Philip Mirowski and Esther-Mirjam Sent, 69–108. Chicago: University of Chicago Press.

Smith, Sean M., and Karen L. Prestegaard. 2005. "Hydraulic Performance of a Morphology-Based Stream Channel Design." *Water Resources Research* no. 41 (W11413).

Soar, Phillip J. 2000. "Channel Restoration Design for Meandering Rivers." PhD diss., University of Nottingham, Nottingham.

Soto-Laveaga, Gabriele. 2009. *Jungle Laboratories: Mexican Peasants, National Projects, and the Making of the Pill*. Durham, N.C.: Duke University Press.

Star, Susan Leigh. 1989. *Regions of the Mind: Brain Research and the Quest for Scientific Certainty*. Stanford, Calif.: Stanford University Press.

Star, Susan Leigh, and James B. Griesemer. 1989. "Institutional Ecology, 'Translation,' and Boundary Objects: Amateurs and Professionals in Berkeley's Museum of Vertebrate Zoology, 1907–39." *Social Studies of Science* 19(3): 387–420.

Sudduth, Elizabeth, Brooke A. Hassett, Peter Cada, and Emily Bernhardt. 2011.

"Testing the Field of Dreams Hypothesis: Functional Responses to Urbanization and Restoration in Stream Ecosystems." *Ecological Applications* 21(6): 1972–88.

Sudduth, Elizabeth, Judy Meyer, and Emily Bernhardt. 2007. "Stream Restoration Practices in the Southeastern United States." *Restoration Ecology* 15(3): 573–83.

Sunder-Rajan, Kaushik. 2006. *Biocapital: The Constitution of Postgenomic Life.* Durham, N.C.: Duke University Press.

Taylor, Peter. 1997. "Appearances Notwithstanding, We Are All Doing Something like Political Ecology." *Social Epistemology* 11(1): 111–27.

Thompson, Douglas M. 2005. "The History of the Use and Effectiveness of Instream Structures in the United States." In *Humans as Geologic Agents*, edited by J. Ehlen, W. C. Haneberg, and R. A. Larson, 35–50. Boulder, Colo.: Geological Society of America Reviews in Engineering Geology.

Thompson, Douglas M., and Gregory N. Stull. 2002. "The Development and Historic Use of Habitat Structures in Channel Restoration in the United States: The Grand Experiment in Fisheries Management." *Géographie physique et quaternaire* 56(1): 45–60.

Todd, Jeffrey W. 1980. "The Wildlife Biologist in the Minerals Industry." *Wildlife Society Bulletin* 8(1): 61–63.

Traweek, Sharon. 1988. *Beamtimes and Lifetimes.* Cambridge, Mass.: Harvard University Press.

Tyfield, David. 2010. "Neoliberalism, Intellectual Property and the Global Knowledge Economy." In *The Rise and Fall of Neoliberalism: The Collapse of an Economic Order?*, edited by Kean Birch and V. Mykhenko, 60–76. London: Zed Books.

Violin, Christy R., Peter Cada, Elizabeth Sudduth, Brooke A. Hassett, David L. Penrose, and Emily Bernhardt. 2011. "Effects of Urbanization and Urban Stream Restoration on the Physical and Biological Structure of Stream Ecosystems." *Ecological Applications* 21(6): 1932–49.

Vira, B., and W. M. Adams. 2009. "Ecosystem Services and Conservation Strategy: Beware the Silver Bullet." *Conservation Letters* 2:158–62.

Walker, Jeremy, and Melinda Cooper. 2011. "Genealogies of Resilience: From Systems Ecology to the Political Economy of Crisis Adaptation." *Security Dialogue* 42(2): 143–60.

Watts, Michael J. 1985. "Social Theory and Environmental Degradation: The Case of Sudano-Sahelian West Africa." In *Desert Development: Man and Technology in Sparselands*, edited by Y. Gradus, 14–32. Dordrecht: Reidel.

———. 1987. "Drought, Environment and Food Security: Some Reflections on Peasants, Pastoralists and Commodification in Dryland West Africa." In *Drought and Hunger in Africa*, edited by M. Glantz, 171–212. Cambridge: Cambridge University Press.

———. 2000. "Political Ecology." In *A Companion to Economic Geography*, edited by Trevor Barnes and Eric Sheppard, 257–75. Oxford: Blackwell.

Watts, Michael J., and James McCarthy. 1997. "Nature as Artifice, Nature as Artefact:

Development, Environment and Modernity in the Late Twentieth Century." In *Geographies of Economies*, edited by Roger Lee and Jane Wills, 71–86. London: Arnold.

White, R. J., and O. M. Brynildson. 1967. *Guidelines for Management of Trout Stream Habitat*. Madison, Wis.: Department of Natural Resources.

Wilcock, Peter R., J. J. Clark, Derek B. Booth, Janine Castro, Craig Fischenich, P. Grams, Karen Gran, J. Steven Kite, G. M. Kondolf, J. D. G. Marr, James MacBroom, J. Moore, R. Newbury, M. A. Palmer, M. E. Power, J. C. Schmidt, F. Douglas Shields, and V. Voller. In preparation. "Stream Restoration Training: Status and Proposal for a New Approach." *Journal of the American Water Resources Association*. Forthcoming.

Wild and Scenic Rivers Act. 1968. Pub. L. No. 90-542. 16 USC 1271–87.

Williams, G. W. 1978. "Bankful Discharge of Rivers." *Water Resources Research* 14:1141–54.

Wilshusen, Peter. 2009. "Shades of Social Capital: Elite Persistence and the Everyday Politics of Community Forestry in Southeastern Mexico." *Environment and Planning A* 41(2): 389–406.

Wolman, M. Gordon, and Ran Gerson. 1978. "Relative Scales of Time and Effectiveness of Climate in Watershed Geomorphology." *Earth Surface Processes* 3:189–208.

Wolman, M. Gordon, and J. P. Miller. 1960. "Magnitude & Frequency of Forces in Geomorphic Processes." *Journal of Geology* 68:57–74.

INDEX

GEOGRAPHIES OF JUSTICE AND SOCIAL TRANSFORMATION

Printed in the USA
CPSIA information can be obtained
at www.ICGtesting.com
LVHW030713251023
761974LV00009B/146

Batch 761974LV00009B

761974LVX00140B	9781638231394	How to Attract Money, Revised Edition
CASE	5.00X8.00	100 <A> 0.375 GLOSS (1)
761974LVX00141B	9781645940470	1900 or, The Last President: The Original
CASE	5.50X8.50	56 <AA> 0.3125 GLOSS (5)
761974LVX00142B	9781645941569	The Machine Stops
CASE	5.50X8.50	60 <AA> 0.3125 GLOSS (1)
761974LVX00143B	9781645941071	The Professor's House
CASE	5.50X8.50	174 <D> 0.5625 GLOSS (1)
761974LVX00144B	9780062573254	Five Little Pigs
CASE	5.50X8.50	288 <I> 0.875 GLOSS (1)
761974LVX00145B	9781636411804	Bruchko: The Astonishing True Story of a
CASE	6.00X9.00	224 <F> 0.6875 GLOSS (1)
761974LVX00146B	9781603868907	Trustful Surrender to Divine Providence:
CASE	6.00X9.00	52 <AAA> 0.25 GLOSS (1)